Forex Trading Strategy

How to Invest with the Simplest and Most Profitable Strategy to Make Money in Trading Stocks, Options, Forex, and ETFs in 2019/2020 in Just 30 Minutes Per Day

Jim Livermore

Table of Contents

Stick to One Trading Style

Start with a Demo Account

Stick to a Limited Number of Currency Pairs

Always Use Stop-Loss Orders and Limit Risk

Don't Trade Based on Emotion

Don't Neglect Fundamental Analysis

Be Informed and Educated

Stick to Your Plan

Conclusion + FREE GIFT

Introduction

Congratulations on purchasing *Forex Trading Strategy: How to Invest with the Simplest and Most Profitable Strategy to Make Money in Trading Stocks, Options, Forex, and ETFs in 2019/2020 in Just 30 Minutes Per Day* and thank you for doing so!

Forex trading is one of the most exciting ways that you can build your own wealth and independent income. It can be fast-paced and exciting; however, there is a Forex trading strategy for nearly every type of mindset. In this book, which is intended for beginners, we are going to explain in basic and easily understandable terms what Forex is all about. You are going to learn how currencies are traded, where they are traded, as well as how you can get involved with Forex trading.

We'll discuss the amount of money that you need to get started, as well as how much you can realistically expect to make. You will learn how the markets work and different approaches to trading that can be used and fit with any lifestyle. We'll explain how you can trade part-time with relatively low risk, or if you want to become a full-time trader that earns fast profits, we'll discuss that, too.

The following chapters will discuss the following topics:

- We begin with a description of Forex markets and their history. Our introduction will assume that the reader has little to no background in Forex but is eager to learn. You'll find out where the Forex markets came from, how they developed, as well as how they've opened up for individual traders.

- Forex vs. Stocks: In this chapter, we'll compare Forex trading with stock trading. The one that you prefer is largely a matter of personal taste, but we'll discuss the pros and cons of each trading platform.

- Setting up a trading account: Learn how to get started with this quick start guide that will teach you how to find a broker to do your Forex trades, as well as trading platforms that are available for desktop and mobile.

- Forex Trading Fundamentals: Learn about pips, currency pairs, lot sizes, and more. We'll break down the basics of the Forex markets so that you can move from beginner to expert in the shortest amount of time.

- Majors and Exotics: Learn which currency pairs are traded frequently and how they are classified.

- Trading Strategies: In this chapter, we'll review the basic trading techniques that are the most popular. This will allow you to determine whether you want to earn short term profits using a "day trading" style, or whether you want a more relaxed part-time approach. We will also teach you about candlestick charts and indicators.

- Fundamental vs. Technical Analysis: In this chapter, we'll discuss the general similarities and differences between fundamental and technical analysis, as well as the various tools that each approach utilizes in Forex trading.

- Trading Plan: Every good trader has a trading plan, and not having one is often the difference between success and failure.

- Forex Trading Secrets: In this chapter, we'll present tips for successful Forex trading.

There are plenty of books on Forex trading on the market—thanks again for choosing this one! Every effort was made to ensure it is full of as much useful information as possible. Please enjoy!

Chapter 1: What Is Forex?

Anyone who's been interested in trading on the financial markets is constantly seeing the term Forex. It's plastered everywhere, and you probably see ads for it on YouTube and other sites that you visit. Although cryptocurrency has grabbed some of the hype of late, Forex trading remains immensely popular. So what is the buzz all about?

In this chapter, we hope to answer this question for the beginner. We're assuming that our readers are new to the world of Forex, and so the reader only has a vague notion of what Forex is about, if you understand it at all. If you do know a bit about Forex, consider this first chapter a review.

Let's get started with the basic definitions:

What Is Forex?

Forex is a shorthand term for *foreign exchange*. In short, it's a market where currencies are traded against each other. They are traded in pairs, for the simple fact that currencies are exchanged for one another in pairs in the real world. If you are traveling from the United States to Europe, you are going to trade dollars for Euros in order to be able to conduct financial transactions in Europe. Likewise, if you are traveling to Canada, you'll need to trade your money for Canadian dollars.

This need, to have local currency in order to engage in financial transactions, is something that extends to the world of business. If you are a Japanese company selling goods to Americans, you are going to get paid in dollars— but to utilize the money at home, you'll need to convert it into Japanese Yen.

Hence, currency trading is a part of everyday life, from the scale of a single individual all the way up to large corporations and even governments. Each nation-state (or in the case of the European Union, an open trading zone with free travel between nations) has its own currency that they use to engage in local financial transactions. Moving across borders or doing business across borders means that you'll have to exchange one currency for another.

And in order to do this, there has to be a standardized way that currencies are exchanged. In other words, we have to know how many Euros a dollar can buy, or how many dollars a Japanese Yen can purchase.

You could just make a law and decree that a Euro was worth two U.S. dollars, but that would not be a realistic way to deal with the issues surrounding currency exchange. However, that would be like saying a pound of beef was forever fixed at $3 a pound. A better way to manage it is to recognize that, like anything else related to finance, currency exchange is something that exists in a market. In other words, supply and demand changes with time, based on many factors.

These factors can range from simple changes in individual behavior, like a sudden flood of people traveling from Canada to the United States, causing a rise in demand for U.S. dollars relative to Canadian dollars—or it could stem from trade. The U.S. is a net importer of goods from overseas, meaning that dollars are flowing out of the country by large amounts—but the actual values of this dollar flow are constantly fluctuating and changing with time. In other cases, countries might buy foreign government debt. For example, China, Japan, and Russia have bought large amounts of U.S. government debt.

There can even be demand for a currency because of macroeconomic circumstances. The U.S. dollar remains the world's so-called "reserve" currency. Its viewed as always having inherent value, backed by the power of the U.S. government. If there are economic problems in some other country—it could be anyone—people might want more dollars to hedge their risks. If you were living in Russia, the value of Rubles might be suspect, or there might be high inflation—but one thing you can count on is that dollars are always going to have value (of course, we are talking in the near term; what the world will be like in 30–50 years, we can't predict).

No matter the reason, money is always moving back and forth across the border—and the supply and demand of various currencies are constantly fluctuating. And what is one of the most basic rules of economics? If demand is outstripping supply, then prices will rise. On the other hand, if demand is weak, then prices will drop.

Currencies Are Traded in Pairs

This is something we are going to come back to again and again throughout this book, as it's a central fact of Forex trading. Currencies are always traded in pairs, one currency against another. So although a currency, in some sense, has an absolute value within the borders of the country (that is, you can buy a pound of beef or a dozen eggs with this many dollars or Euros), when it comes to international trading, it is only the value of one currency against another that counts.

Therefore, in the Forex markets, you can trade *currency pairs*. We will get into the specifics of this later and how it works, but you can either buy or sell a currency pair, which simply means that you are exchanging one currency for another. You are hoping that the value of the currency that you are holding as a part of this transaction is going to rise in value against the other member of the currency pair so that you'll be able to exchange it back later and have more money in your own currency.

It's that simple. Currency trading is a very basic concept, and this is one of the reasons that it attracts so many investors and traders. As compared with stocks, currency trading is incredibly simple. You don't have to worry about company earnings reports, price to earnings ratios, or pour over the financial statements of the company. Currency trading is about one thing and one thing only – the relative demand of one currency with respect to another.

In the previous section, we mentioned some of the factors that can impact supply, demand, and pricing for currencies.

Since the introduction of "retail" Forex markets (that is, Forex trading open to the general public), another factor has been introduced that impacts the supply and demand of currencies—and that is simply the traders themselves.

In today's world, the whims of traders, including large institutional traders, can have a large impact on the supply and demand, and hence the relative values of different currencies. Traders alone can now drive up the value of the Euro with respect to the Japanese Yen, or traders rushing for the exits could cause the Australian Dollar to lose value against the Canadian dollar. Moves by large institutions, which can buy or sell huge blocks of currency in a single transaction, can have a massive impact on the markets.

A large part of currency exchange in today's world is speculation—and probably, that is what is drawing you to the Forex markets. Basically, traders are speculating on price movements of one currency against another and hoping to book profits by trading the currencies at the best possible times.

An Overview of the Forex Market

Let's take a step back and get some understanding of how the Forex market is structured, and who the major players are. The first thing to know about the Forex market is that it is what financial experts call an over-the-counter market. What this means is that there is not a formal exchange where trading takes place. To understand what we are getting at, we can think about stocks and options. There are formal, centralized exchanges where stocks are sold, such as the New York Stock exchange. Options are traded on the Chicago Options exchange.

Currency is not traded like that. It's traded over what is known as a broker-dealer network. While there are major cities where trading takes place, such as New York, London, or Tokyo, currency trading involves over-the-counter trades run by broker-dealers.

These are companies that complete financial transactions on behalf of investors. So, you open an account with a broker-dealer, and you place orders with them, which they carry out for you. Of course, they take a small fee for doing so, that the way these fees add up over the large numbers of transactions they process is how they make money. In the case of Forex, broker-dealers can arrange trades between different individuals, but they are also able to trade currency with large institutions like banks.

There are several big players in currency exchange markets. Banks are the oldest and longest-running players in the Forex markets. This can include central banks as well as commercial banks, that will exchange large amounts of one currency for another as the need arises. Investment banking companies are also involved in currency exchange, and large corporations that do business internationally will also be doing a large number of currency exchanges. Hedge funds are trading Forex to make profits, and finally, there are "retail" investors and retail Forex dealers. Basically, a retail investor is a small, individual investor such as yourself. A retail Forex dealer is just a broker that retail investors use to implement trades.

The main role of the Forex market is to set exchange values between currencies. So as we've alluded to earlier, the market would set the value of Euros against the Great British Pound, or against the U.S. Dollar, to use two examples. If a currency is a free-float currency, which is what most of them are, then the values of currency with respect to other currencies is determined solely by market forces – supply and demand. Some currencies are known as fixed float currencies. The two main examples are the Chinese Yuan and the Indian Rupee. A fixed float currency is one that has its value pegged to some specific value, usually another currency like the U.S. Dollar.

Although there isn't a formal exchange like the New York Stock Exchange and trading is done over the counter, there are several financial centers where trading occurs. This includes many large cities such as New York, London, Sydney, Toronto, Hong Kong, and Tokyo. Since the market is global, trading goes on 24 hours a day during business days. That means that you have six days a week, 24 hours a day when you can trade. Trading begins when the markets open in New Zealand every Monday morning, local time, which is in the afternoon on Sunday in the United States. It continues until markets close in New York on Fridays.

This means that the markets are highly liquid—that is, you can trade all the time and quickly convert your investment into cash. The Forex markets have grown incomprehensibly large, reaching a daily trading volume of more than $5 trillion by the end of 2016. This is much larger than the trading volume on any stock market, which ranges around $200 billion per day.

Since Forex trading is "over-the-counter," it is lightly regulated as opposed to stock market investing. This can be beneficial to traders, as it can make it easier to trade, and you can use high amounts of leverage (but remember that leverage can work for or against you).

The Bretton Woods Agreements

The world of currency exchange was heavily influenced by the Bretton Woods agreements. The first agreement occurred in 1944 and was made among the allied nations in the Second World War as an effort to establish a smooth currency trading system once the war ended. The agreement mainly focused on the behaviors of each nation's central banks and how each currency was related to the U.S. Dollar, which at that time was establishing itself as the world's so-called reserve currency.

Since the U.S. Dollar was deemed the reserve currency, all other currencies were to trade at a fixed rate against the dollar. If market conditions changed the rate, the countries that were parties to the agreement agreed to have their central banks buy up the currency as needed to keep the rates constant.

The Bretton Woods agreement effectively meant that most nations were abandoning the gold standard, which had been in place for currencies prior to this agreement. The gold standard meant that a given currency could be exchanged for a fixed amount of gold, therefore pegging its value to gold. Under the new system, the value of a currency was basically pegged to the U.S. dollar. This created several problems, such as the increasing role of the International Monetary Fund, which served to bail countries out if their currency collapsed in value.

The dollar was still pegged to gold, but economic problems in the United States led the Nixon administration to change the amount of gold you could get with a dollar. This created a "gold rush" where people began exchanging dollars for gold. This happened out of fear because the Nixon administration kept reducing the amount of gold that a dollar could buy. So people, fearing that the dollar was losing value, wanted to get gold while they could still do it before the value dropped.

The Nixon administration then took the U.S. dollar completely off the gold standard. That opened up the price of gold to the free market, and prices of gold skyrocketed.

These events took place in the early 1970s, and so 1971 is taken as the date at which the Bretton Woods system basically collapsed. The U.S. dollar has remained the world's reserve currency, but now rather than being pegged to a certain amount of gold, everything was free-floating. These developments eventually opened the door to retail Forex trading.

Banks Dominated Forex Until 1999

In the decades that followed, currency trading remained limited to banks and large traders that could move millions or tens of millions of units of currency in a single trade. Trading was slow and monolithic, with trades occurring once a day. Individual traders were not able to buy and sell currency for profits the way they are today, although you could have purchased your own actual currency and saved it in your mattress, hoping that the value would go up when you exchanged it back for dollars at a later date.

So until the late 1990s, the banks traded currency among themselves. This involved both central banks run by governments and large commercial banks. Some other large players were also able to engage in currency trading.

In the 1990s, the internet was commercialized and rapidly evolving. It soon exploded and began to play a large role in the economy, including stock trading, as brokers began to move online. This opened the door to a massive increase in an individual stock, options, and commodity traders who were able to use their own computers to engage in lighting fast trading.

At this time, some people had an ingenious idea – why not open up currency trading to the retail market?

The way this was done is people began to set up what is known as Forex dealers. These dealers acted as middlemen so that they could obtain the large amounts of currency needed to make retail trading available to the public.

The way this worked (and still works today) is that a Forex dealer would trade with the banks. They buy large amounts of currency, which they then make available to the public at large. Then, when people enter into a trade, either the dealer will match you up to another trader that wants to take the opposite position in the trade, or they will take the position themselves.

The old ways of currency trading are still going on. So banks are still trading currencies with other banks (and across borders, so a bank in Germany might trade currency with a bank in London). However, today, the market has grown to encompass Forex dealers and the general public ("retail investors").

Types of Forex Dealers

Forex dealers (also known as FX dealers) come in two flavors. An FX dealer is a company that has been set up to act as an intermediary between the general public and the banks. If the dealer is known as "STP," this means that it is a straight-through processing FX dealer. That means that the dealer will match you to another trader (or even a bank) that will take the other side of your trade. In other words, if you buy Euros, the other party they match you to is willing to sell you the Euros for dollars. This all happens by the computer automatically and instantly, so you are not going to know who is on the other side of the trade, and it's completely irrelevant, anyway.

If an FX dealer is a "dealing desk," this means the dealer will take the other end of the trade.

Generally speaking, as a small trader, you are going to be dealing with STP dealers. Dealing desks are used for large trades of $10 million or more. Those types of large trades are generally not suitable for STP dealers, because as you can imagine, it's harder to find someone to take the other side of a $10 million trade than it is to find someone to take the other side of a $5,000 or $500 trade. So dealers or banks can step in for the large trades.

As a practical matter, these issues won't impact most readers.

Background and Philosophy

Like you, I have been involved in many different types of trading. I had to feel my way around the markets until I found trading methods that worked so that I could build a financially independent existence based on an income from trading. I've tried it all, day trading, swing trading, and options trading. While I still use options trading to build wealth, I have found that Forex trading is the easiest way to make money among all the different options available.

My basic philosophy of trading is to focus on discipline and planning. We will talk more about this in Chapters 8 & 9 of this book, but following a set of rules or guidelines, and acting within a trading plan are the keys to success as a trader. It's very easy to get caught up in the emotion of trading. We've all been there, and I've made many mistakes along the way to learning how to trade effectively.

It's important that you understand the differences between trading and investing. First of all, neither is better than the other – they are just different ways of approaching the financial markets. Unfortunately, many investors have attitudes that they are smarter and more careful, and they look down on traders who they view as gamblers. Nothing could be further from the truth.

Investing, as the name implies, is putting your money into an asset that you expect to appreciate over the long term. That means investing money in a company for ten, twenty, or even thirty years. You are basically making yourself a part of the company and hoping to build wealth with the company as it grows.

Trading is a method of making short-term profits. Rather than being gambling, trading is a for-profit business. Of course, some people are not going to succeed at trading – businesses in every industry fail. Trading uses the short-term price fluctuations of financial securities in order to make profits. Some people call this "speculating" because you are anticipating rising or falling prices of different financial assets that you hope to profit from. Although investors look down on this and make comparisons to "tulip bulbs" and other crazes, trading is based on trading real financial assets and is not a game.

Can you gamble as a trader? Of course, you can. Some people engage in trading without actually thinking about what they are doing or planning it out. In that case, you are gambling, taking a roll of the dice "hoping" that the value of a certain stock or currency is going to go up.

Trading is not about that. As a trader, you are going to approach this as a serious business. You will plan out your trades, set goals, and manage your risk. A trader is no more a gambler than a restaurant owner. Most restaurants fail, so does that make the food industry gambling? Of course, not.

In this book, besides explaining the basics of the Forex markets, we hope to teach you what you need to know in order to establish a solid trading plan so that you can follow in my footsteps and build a sustainable and profitable Forex trading business.

In the next chapter, we will consider Forex trading against stock trading, so you can decide for yourself if you want to do one or the other, or trade within both markets.

Chapter 2: Forex vs. Stocks

One of the questions a new trader faces is what markets to invest in. Stocks remain one of the most popular ways to invest and grow wealth—and with good reason. The fact is, despite the frequent ups and downs of the markets, over time, stocks are proven to be a good way to generate large amounts of wealth.

In this chapter, we will look at the question of Forex vs. stocks and address the issue of picking one or the other. Of course, they are not necessarily mutually exclusive. If you have the time and ability to learn, follow, and manage two completely different markets, it's certainly possible to do so. However, for beginning traders, it's probably better to stick with one type of trading at least for six months. After you have developed a reasonable level of mastery, then you may find branching out a little easier.

Forex Is Easier for Beginners

Forex has a reputation for being a high risk. In fact, from the perspective of many financial experts, Forex might even seem like its nothing more than a gambling casino. However, the reality is much different Forex is actually easier for most beginning traders once they understand the concepts of currency pairs. There is far less information to worry about and less you have to manage. You can also use the volatility of the Forex markets to your advantage more easily than you can with stocks.

With stocks, you have to be closely following different companies and keeping track of a large amount of information. You'll have to know how to read balance sheets and what everything means in financial statements. You'll have to keep close tabs on company management and product releases, as well as any news about a company coming out day-to-day that could have a large impact on stock prices. And you'll have to keep track of macroeconomic and political news.

Of course, the economy can impact currency trading, but overall, the total amount of information you have to keep track of and learn about is much smaller with Forex. You'll need to keep up with basic financial news, and most importantly, with the international economic and political situations. But there are no financial statements to pour over, and with currency, there is always the possibility of just holding on until things reverse and go your way.

The skills that you learn trading Forex are easily translatable to other markets. So you can learn a great deal about candlestick charts, price movements, and technical indicators in the simpler world of Forex – and you'll be able to translate this information to the world of stocks or options trading, or even commodities and precious metals.

Forex Is 24-Hours-a-Day Trading

With stocks, you can trade during the "trading day," which is roughly 9:30 AM until 4 PM eastern time. Forex is not constrained to New York City; it's a global market. That means that you can trade any time of day or night during the business week, and that business week does the stretch from Sunday through Friday afternoon, so you basically have six days a week, 24 hours a day to trade. The markets are truly global, and so the markets are highly liquid and flexible. You can get in and out of trades at an opportune moment.

The 24-hour nature of the Forex market removes many of the constraints faced by day traders on the stock market. Because of the sensitivity of their positions, a day trader can literally get wiped out if they were to hold their positions overnight. The first minutes of trading at the next opening can cause them to lose thousands of dollars in the blink of an eye.

In Forex, you are not worried about a frantic activity like that over the "opening" because strictly speaking, other than the opening of the markets on Sunday afternoon New York time in New Zealand, there is no opening bell. You can hold out if a position is not working out for you, provided that holding out is the reasonable thing to do. The point is that the 24-hours-a-day nature of the truly global Forex markets means that you have a lot more flexibility on Forex as compared to the stock markets.

And the 24-hours-a-day markets mean something else – basic flexibility. If you are trading stocks, you might have a "day job," and you won't be able to follow the markets that closely. But with Forex, the situation is totally different. You can trade whenever it's convenient for you. The fact that the markets are open 24 hours a day means that you can even engage in activities like day trading while still working a full-time job during the day. For this reason alone, many people opt for Forex trading.

Liquidity and Trading Volume

Two of the leading reasons that Forex is preferred by many traders as compared to stocks are liquidity and trading volume. As we noted in the previous chapter, the Forex markets see $5 trillion or more in trades per day. This compares to around $220 billion per day on the NY Stock Exchange, and $100 billion per day on the NASDAQ.

What this means in practical terms, is it's very easy to find buyers and sellers to help you get in and out of your positions quickly. The high liquidity of Forex markets makes day trading easier, and it even permits trading on very short time intervals using a method called "scalping."

Even if you are not into the idea of day trading or scalping, the increased liquidity of the Forex markets is a definite advantage for any trader. Prices on financial markets can move fast, and so it's reassuring knowing that with Forex, you will be able to find a buyer pretty quickly.

Limited Options Actually Makes Forex Easier

This might seem counter-intuitive, but one of the advantages of Forex over the stock market is there are a limited number of trading opportunities. In fact, the vast majority of trading is centered around a few major currencies like the Euro, U.S. Dollar, and Japanese Yen.

As a trader, this makes life a lot simpler from your perspective. Rather than having to pour through hundreds of stocks looking for the right trade to get into, there are a small handful of possibilities on the Forex markets.

This can help by just keeping your mind from being overwhelmed. Of course, this cuts both ways, a large number of stocks that are available (there are 2,800 companies on the New York Stock Exchange and 3,300 companies on NASDAQ) means that it's easier to find investments that are personally tailored to your needs and interests. But the fact is most people that have that kind of interest in stocks and companies are more likely to be long-term investors, rather than traders who are looking to make short-term profits.

Traders are not the type to really care about the details of what they are trading. They are only interested in short-term profit potential. So a volatile stock is going to be preferred over a stock that has a product they like or management team that they admire. If you are interested in the products some company is producing, then you're probably going to want to sink your money in that company for ten years. Many people invest in companies like Apple or Amazon for this reason.

But if you are only interested in price movements, the company is not really all that relevant. So why even worry about companies themselves at all. With Forex, there are a limited number of major currencies that you can trade and make profits with; in fact, as we'll see, the vast majority of the trading volume is centered on a rather small number of currencies. That means that you can find the trades you want to get into rather easily, by only looking at a few different currency pairs instead of pouring through hundreds of stocks trying to find the right one.

It's really not fair to say that one way is better than another. It comes down to personal taste, and the reality is that some people actually prefer the huge variety on the stock market, and even if they are only attempting to make profits from price movements, they still find finance, business, and corporations to be of interest. For others, the specific nature of the underlying financial asset is not all that important. Instead, the focus for them is simply the price movements and the potential for making profits in a risky environment.

Later we are going to be talking a little bit about what is known as technical analysis. You don't have to be some kind of math or financial whiz to trade Forex, but many people who are interested in Forex or even day trading stocks enjoy pouring overpricing charts and studying price movements of financial instruments.

Forex provides ample opportunity to do this, and in fact, it comes with the territory. A Forex trader has to have at least some familiarity with candlestick charts, moving averages, and technical indicators. These tools are used by traders when they study charts so that they can estimate trends in pricing and coming price changes. The tools can be used with any financial instrument; in fact, candlestick charts were developed in Japan a couple of centuries ago in order to track changes in rice prices on the markets.

Massive Leverage Is Possible with Forex

One of the major advantages of Forex on stock and even options trading is the ability to use massive leverage. If you are a day or swing trader on the stock market, you can use

2:1 leverage. That means you can basically borrow from the broker to make larger trades than you would be able to make using your own money. If you have access to 2:1 leverage, the broker will lend you enough money to double it, so if you put up $5,000, you can make a $10,000 trade. Of course, when you sell the shares, you have to pay the broker back the $5,000 you borrowed.

As you might imagine, leverage allows you to make a lot more profits than you could otherwise. Let's say that you were able to enter a trade on a certain stock that made a $2 a share gain in a single day. If you had $5,000 cash, and the stock was trading at $40 a share, you would be able to buy 125 shares. So your total profit would be $2 x 125 = $250. Not bad for a day's work, but consider using leverage.

On the stock market, you would be able to access 2:1 leverage, so you'd be able to buy 250 shares, and make a total of $500 profit. As we noted above, the trade works because the broker would lend you the extra $5,000 so that you could buy $10,000 worth of stock. Then, the trade goes as follows. You buy 250 shares with the $10,000. Then, when the stock price rises by $2 a share, you can sell the shares for $10,500. You return the $5,000 to the broker, and you pocket the $500 profit. Leverage has allowed you to earn $250 over and above what you could have earned.

Note that on the stock market, to use leverage, you have to open a margin account. This might have a few special requirements, one of which is that you have to deposit $2,000 cash typically in order to open the account.

Now, imagine if you had 10:1 leverage. On the same trade, you could buy 10 times as much stock. That is, if you had $5,000 in your account, your broker would loan you enough money to buy 10 times as much – or $50,000 worth of stock. At $40 a share, you would be able to buy 1,250 shares. If the stock rose in price by $2 a share, you'd make $2,500 in profits. You could sell the stock, and then just return the $45,000 you borrowed from the broker.

We can go crazy with the concept. Suppose that you had the ability to access 50:1 leverage. So with $5,000, you could spend $5,000 x 50 = $250,000 to buy shares of stock. In that case, you would be able to buy 6,250 shares of a stock trading at $40 a share, and if it rose by $2 a share, you would make a profit of $12,500! When you sold the shares on the market for a profit, then you would simply return the $245,000 to the broker.

That crazy situation is the kind of leverage you have access to on the Forex markets. Of course, that doesn't mean that just because you can use $5,000 to leverage a $250,000 trade that you should do it, but the point here is that you do have access to that amount of leverage on Forex. This is one reason that traders find Forex to be more attractive than trading stocks. The leverage gives traders a lot of power that they would not have otherwise.

Remember that leverage can cut both ways. For example, let's return to our example of using 10:1 leverage. In that case, we were able to borrow $45,000 on our $5,000 account to buy 1,250 shares. But what if instead of gaining $2 a share, it lost $2 a share. That would mean that we'd end up losing $2,500. Of course, the broker doesn't take the loss for you. When you have losses, you have to pay back the $45,000 that you borrowed, no matter what. So that would mean that our account dropped in value from $5,000 to $2,500 on the trade. If the stock dropped $4 a share, then you'd be wiped out.

Now, consider a $5 drop-in share price. That would not only wipe out your account; it would mean there was an extra $1,250 in losses. You can't take that out of the borrowed broker proceeds. This situation results in what is known as a margin call. The broker would sell your position, and then the margin call means that the broker would be demanding you pay up the $1,250 in extra losses.

There are ways to protect yourself against losses like that and margin calls, but we are using this example to illustrate the concept. Later, we will talk about how to protect yourself from risk and the exact steps to use. Smart traders don't let themselves get into those kinds of situations in the first place – so you need to have an awareness that this can happen.

Although we used examples of buying stocks, the exact same process works on the Forex markets. Leverage on Forex markets in the United States is 50:1. In some countries such as Australia, Britain, and many others, there is actually 100:1 leverage. However, many of those countries are considering adopting the U.S. standard of 50:1 leverage. But the bottom line is not to use leverage recklessly, and you want to avoid getting in situations involving margin calls.

To sum up, however, the greater availability of leverage on the Forex markets is seen as a major advantage to traders. As a small trader, being able to use 50:1 leverage will allow you to make outsized trades that make it easier to start making profits without having to invest a lot of money upfront. Think about the power of leverage, using only small amounts to invest. A mere $50 investment in the Forex market can let you control 10,000 units of currency when leverage is used.

Its claimed by some that a $5,000 investment can lead to a $100,000 per year income. This is possible largely because of the large amount of leverage that is available on Forex, provided that you trade methodically and carefully. The specific amount of margin available may vary from broker to broker, so do your research before you select a broker to go with for your trading.

Big Players Are Less Able to Control Forex Markets

On the stock market, it's possible for large hedge funds and institutional investors to make the markets move. They can dump a large number of shares, causing the price of a given stock to drop suddenly—or they can start buying up shares, causing the price of the stock to rise.

These kinds of actions by the big players are not as feasible on the Forex markets, due to the simple fact that the Forex markets have such a large volume. The paradox is that the Forex markets have far more volume than the stock market, but this makes the Forex markets far more "democratic" and less susceptible to manipulation by big traders.

For this reason, many retail traders prefer Forex to the stock market. The situation can be described as one with a level playing field. Since the markets are far harder to manipulate, the small retail investor has more protection than they would on the stock market, when the kinds of price shifts caused by big players are under consideration.

Forex Offers Lower Transaction Costs

One of the impacts of the higher levels of liquidity in a financial market is there are tighter spreads and lower transaction costs. What does this mean to you in practical terms? The bottom line here is that your costs of trading are going to be lower on the Forex markets than they are going to be trading stocks. In most cases, you are going to have to pay for spreads, and you'll pay a large commission per trade on the stock market. On Forex, in most cases, there are not any commissions. So your only fees are going to be related to spreads.

Forex Is Less Regulated

Of course, we don't want to live in the wild west; some level of regulation is good. However, remember that the stock markets are very tightly regulated. To be a day trader on the stock market, you have to open a margin account and deposit $25,000 cash. These are requirements that are set by law. And if you are not an official day trader but you make a few day trades just out of the need to make a profit on your stocks, you will be designated a day trader and either be required to pony up the $25,000 or suspend your trading. We aren't talking about some kind of fine, of course; you would be able to use the $25,000 in order to trade stocks. But do you want to be in a position where you have to come up with money of that magnitude because you've made a few day trades?

Forex markets are far more flexible. They are loosely regulated, and globalized. This offers advantages to the small trader so that you have a lot less to worry about as far as regulations and rules are concerned.

Forex Offers a Narrow Focus

Forex traders have fewer variables to consider. Earlier, we touched on this when discussing a large amount of study that is necessary to consider investing in companies and a large number of companies that are traded on stock markets as opposed to the small number of currencies that make up the vast majority of Forex trading.

There are more advantages to this. Specifically, when you are studying a company to invest in or trade, there is going to be a wide range of variables that you have to consider. A company is not just influenced by what the company does or who its management team is, it's influenced by competitors that can make its stock go up or down if they beat it in the market or come out with better products.

The company will also be influenced by trends in the sector. So you not only have to know the company that you are investing in, you have to know all about the company's competition and what they are doing in order to make sound investments. And, you'll have to know about what's going on in the entire sector or industry. For example, if you are looking at pharmaceutical companies to invest in, you'll have to know what drug patents they all have, who is getting new drug patents that could make the company you are interested in worthless, what the FDA is doing that could impact the value of the stock, and what laws congress might be passing that could have a large impact on the pharmaceutical industry.

On top of all of this, you would have to be tracking the economy at large.

In other words, when investing in stocks, there is a wide focus. Day traders may be able to get away without having a wide focus, but even swing traders need to have a wide focus and know what the bigger picture is. Any long-term investor needs to have a wide focus and a deep dive into the companies' fortunes.

In contrast, Forex is really only about two things – the current economic and political situation. Something like trade (to use a recent example) might impact the currency markets, or GDP numbers could have an impact. In other words, your focus when it comes to the Forex markets is narrow rather than wide.

Forex Requires Less Startup Capital

Due to the high amount of leverage that is available, Forex trading requires less startup capital than stock market investing. As we discussed above, with as little as $50, you can control large amounts of currency. In the stock market, with $50, you would only be able to control one share of a middle of the road company. Investing in top companies like Apple, Netflix, and Amazon would be something you'd be dreaming about.

So you can start investing in Forex with hardly any cash on hand (at least in theory, check to see if your broker-dealer has any specific deposit requirements to get started). On the stock market, you are going to need thousands of dollars to get started and realistically make profits. Even to open a margin account, you need to deposit at least $2,000 – just to get started. In most cases, on a per share, basic swing or day traders are talking about making small amounts of money. That means that in order to make real levels of profit – job quitting money – you have to be able to buy a large amount of shares every time you enter into a trade. With Forex, it is just a lot easier to get rolling with smaller amounts of cash. You can keep that $5,000 investment to earn $100,000 a year as a basic rule of thumb in mind.

For this reason, many new traders are drawn to the Forex markets.

Forex vs. Stocks – The Bottom Line

In the end, which path you take is going to be based on your personal preferences and your current financial situation. It will also depend on how much time and energy you have to devote to your trading activities. Some people who are able to pull it off will be able to do both, and you can, too, if that is your inclination—and you are able to do it without getting yourself into financial losses because you were not able to track your investments as closely as you need to. In my view, if you have small amounts of capital and you are just getting started trading, Forex is an easier way to get involved in the world of financial trading with the potential for earning profits.

Chapter 3: Setting Up Your Own Trading Account

Once you've decided to trade Forex and you've gathered some funds together than can be used, the next step in the process is to open a trading account. In order to do this, you will find a broker or dealer that is suitable for your needs. You'll want to find an established and trustworthy dealer that is in your home country. In the United States, many well-known and established stockbrokers such as TD Ameritrade also offer Forex trading. The comfort of being able to trade using a broker like this is that you know it's reliable and that you can trust them. However, there are many other options.

Opening an account for Forex trading is a little more involved than opening a stock trading account, due to the possibilities (real or imagined by authorities) of money laundering. Because of this, broker-dealers are a little more careful about verifying your identity and so forth, but it's not really a big deal to worry about.

Factors to Consider When Opening a Trading Account

There are many things that need to be considered when opening a Forex trading account. The first thing you are going to want to look at is simple ease of use and convenience. These days, many people want to be able to trade using a mobile device such as an iPhone or tablet. Doing so with website-only access can be a bit cumbersome; therefore, many people are searching out dealers that also have mobile apps they can use to execute trades.

Of course, having flexibility is important, too. So traders are also going to be interested in a company that has a desktop, as well as a mobile platform. Most established broker-dealers have both, although, in recent years, there have been some mobile-only stockbrokers emerging. The point is, as a Forex trader, you want to have unfettered access to your account at all times, and you may need to access it on a desktop computer when mobile access is not available for one reason or another.

Another factor that is important is the tools that are made available. Charting is an all-important tool for Forex traders. You need to be able to see price movements in the blink of an eye and be able to recognize trend reversals. So while it sounds basic, you'll want to make sure that your dealer has built-in charts that can be used for the purposes of at least a simple analysis. But, generally speaking, the more tools that are available to the trader, the better.

When looking at charts, a line graph is nice, and it shows you the overall price movement and trend, but it does not convey the level of information that a trader needs to have access to. So you will want to make sure that any broker-dealer that you select also has the ability to make candlestick charts. As we will see later, candlestick charts are important to use in order to determine the trends underlying the current pricing on the charts, and they also play a central role in determining when there is about to be a price reversal. These price or trend reversals (that is, when a rising price is about to become a falling price or vice-versa), are important for traders when determining when to buy or sell currency pairs.

Another tool that your broker needs to make available are technical indicators. You are going to want to be at least able to use moving averages, and also tools like Bollinger bands and the relative strength indicator. Don't worry if you aren't familiar with these tools right now, the important point here is that you have a platform that makes them available. You might not even use all of them in your trading activities, but you are going to want to have them there just in case you need them.

The Basics First

Of course, in any business, whether it's a used car dealer or a Forex broker, one of the first things that come to mind is how long has the company been operating. Of course, new companies are rising all the time, and so this is not a make or break factor. In fact, in recent years, many new stockbrokers have come into existence that has become very popular over a short time period, such as Robin Hood.

But generally speaking, a company that has been in business for a long time period is one that inspires more confidence. You can be assured that the company has some chance of weathering major economic downturns and other events if it's been in business for more than ten years. Some companies, like TD Ameritrade, have been in business for much longer, something that gives us some confidence that the company is mature and stable.

Remember – you are going to be putting your money into an account that is managed by the company. Of course, if the company failed, you can just go trade Forex somewhere else. But what you want to avoid is a situation where the company fails, and you've got $10,000 in your account, and then you have trouble getting it back. While the FDIC insures up to $250,000 in a bank account, you may find that any money you put in a Forex trading account isn't protected. This leads us to the point where looking for established brokers is the preferred route when setting up a new trading account.

Second, you might be interested in the size of the company. Again, this obviously cannot be a hard and fast rule. All companies start somewhere, and many of today's largest corporations like Apple were once operated by two or three individuals in someone's garage. However, as a general rule, a company that has a larger size is going to be one that is preferred to a new startup that only has five employees.

If the company is publicly traded, this is another good sign that it's a brokerage that is – generally speaking – reliable and trustworthy. Of course, we can point to many old, well-established, and large, publicly-traded financial companies that have gone bust in the past. Three of the most famous examples include Lehman Brothers, Bear-Stearns, and Merrill Lynch. These companies were all household names, they were older and mature companies with large numbers of employees, and they were publicly traded. And they all went bust during the 2008 financial crisis. So there are no guarantees in life, but you do have to play odds. And when it comes to probabilities, a company that is publicly traded is a more stable company.

Regulation

Although we prefer a lighter regulatory touch as Forex traders, you do want some regulation; otherwise, you might be taken in by fly-by-night operators that have fancy looking websites. These days it's very easy to create a flashy and professional looking website that can entice people to sign over their money. The website might be based overseas and lack the usual protections that an American based company would offer for investors. A trader is better off actually going with a domain where there is some regulatory touch. The best locations for this are the United States, the United Kingdom, Australia, New Zealand, and Canada.

Creating Your Currency Trading Account

Opening a Forex trading account, for the most part, is no different than anything else you do online. You are going to have basic forms to fill out that asks you general information such as your name, address, and phone number. Other contact information like your email address will probably be required.

To start off, rather than just creating an account, you are going to be required to apply for an account. Remember that Forex trading is considered risky by the authorities in the sense that currency trading could be used for money laundering. So a few hoops are in place that you have to jump through in order to demonstrate that you are who you say you are so that they have some reasonable level of confidence that you are not using Forex trading for this purpose. There are two main things that you have to verify in order to pass the application – the first is that you are a citizen of the country that you are claiming. Second, you are going to have to offer some level of proof of residence—that is, you actually live at the location that you are giving to the broker as your address.

This simply means that you are going to have to upload some documentation. The specifics may vary from broker to broker, but you may be required to send in copies of such items as your driver's license and a current utility bill.

Once this documentation has been sent in, the broker-dealer will review it and get back to you. Assuming that your application is legitimate, the broker will probably approve your application over a time period of 1-3 days. Most applications are approved in about 2 days of time.

Connecting a Bank Account

Once the application is approved, you are nearly ready to go. The final step in the process is to connect a bank account so that you can move funds into an account that your broker sets up for you. And of course, wishing you successful trading, we will want to be able to quickly move profits to a bank account we use so that we can enjoy the fruits of our labors. In order to get started, you will have to wire funds to your broker. As we noted earlier, some brokers might require a minimum deposit. It could be $500 or $1,000. Check with specific brokers or dealers that you are interested in and find out what the specifics are for each particular brokerage.

Once the bank account is connected, the money will move by wire transfer into your account with the brokerage. At this point, you are able to begin trading.

Trading Platform

Many Forex dealers will have their own trading platform, but others will be using meta trader 4, which is trading software designed for Forex markets. Meta trader was first introduced to the Forex community back in 2005. The software is immensely popular among Forex traders, and it's available through many Forex dealers and brokers.

Meta trader 4 includes a server component that is run by the broker. Client software is run by traders on their own desktop machines. More recently, you can download mobile apps to your smartphone or tablet in order to run the platform. The meta trader 4 platforms will allow you to pick currency pairs, view charts and indicators at a glance, and place your trades. It's a very easy platform to use that most people can pick up nearly instantly.

While there are other trading platforms available, one of the benefits of meta trader is the ability of traders to write scripts and even build robots using the platform. This powerful capability enables small, retail traders to automate large parts of their trading activity and to engage in faster computer-controlled trades. This can help traders to earn larger profits by moving in and out of currency positions quickly.

The important part of a trading platform is able to look at charts to spot pricing trends. Depending on what type of strategy you adopt for trading, you will be interested in using these charts – often in real-time – to decide when to place your trades. If your broker is not using meta trader 4, then you are going to want to make sure that whatever software they are using, including if it's in-house developed software, allows the capabilities that you must have so that you can not only make trades quickly but that they are also informed trades.

Chapter 4: The Fundamentals of Forex Trading

In this chapter, we are going to begin reviewing the details of Forex trading. We will start by explaining what is traded and the jargon used in the market. It is quite different than the stock market, and so for many readers, this is going to be new material. Nevertheless, the good thing is that once you learn a few concepts, Forex is quite simple to understand.

Currency Pairs

On the Forex markets, you trade currency pairs. Currencies are grouped together in pairs with the leading member of the pair called the *primary* and the second member of the pair called the *secondary*. When you see quotes, the quote will be listed as primary/secondary.

Each currency has a three-letter abbreviation. You can think of the currency pair as a ticker in the stock exchange. While you might be used to thinking in terms of buying something with dollars, you can buy any currency pair with your Forex account.

As an example, we have:

- EUR/USD

Here, the Euro, abbreviated EUR, is the primary currency. The U.S. Dollar, abbreviated as USD, is the secondary currency. The terms primary and secondary have nothing to do with the value of the currency or its volume. In fact, although the U.S. Dollar is the secondary currency here, the U.S. Dollar makes up one member of a pair in the vast majority of trading on Forex, as you might imagine.

The names used to refer to the two currencies can also go by *base* and *quote*. The base currency pair is the same as the primary. So in the example of EUR/USD, the Euro is the base currency pair. The quote is the secondary, so the USD would be the quote currency.

Pricing of Currency Pairs

Currency pairs are priced according to how much the primary currency is worth in terms of the secondary currency. We can also say that it would be the amount of the secondary currency you would need in order to buy one unit of the primary currency.

Therefore, if you see a quote in the following manner:

EUR/USD = 1.20

That means that it would take $1.20 to buy one Euro, or one Euro is worth a dollar and twenty cents.

You Can Buy or Sell a Currency Pair to Enter a Position

The important thing with currency pairs is to understand how they are traded. This is a major difference in the stock market. On the stock market, if you are interested in a stock, you buy shares of the stock. When you want to exit the position, you sell the stock. On the Forex markets, things are a little bit more complicated.

You can buy or sell a currency pair. The way this works is as follows. When you buy the currency pair, you are buying the primary currency. You will do this if you believe that the value of the primary currency will rise with respect to the value of the secondary currency. Remember that currencies are always compared against one another on the Forex markets, and so these are not absolute values, they are only relative values between the two currencies that are under consideration.

If you buy a currency pair, then you are hoping or anticipating that the primary currency is going to rise in value with respect to the secondary currency. So if you buy the EUR/USD pair, when its quoted at 1.20, you are hoping that it's going to rise to say 1.30, so that you will be able to exit your position by selling the pair for a profit later on. In this way, it's the same as going long on a stock if you want to think in those terms.

So when you are looking at charts, you are going to think in conventional stock market terms. That is, buy low and sell high. You will use the same mentality when you are looking at the charts on the Forex market. In the example below, we are showing an opportunity to buy the EUR/USD pair and then sell it later for a profit.

Euro / U.S. Dollar · 1 · FXCM   1.10390 −0.00002 (−0.00%)

SELL ⟶

BUY

9   03:00   06:00   09:00   12:00   15:00

Selling a Currency Pair: How It Works, and Why You Do It

Of course, since currencies are always quoted in pairs, you might want to bet on the other currency – the secondary – rather than always betting on the primary currency. Conceptually, this can be thought of as "shorting" a stock, but of course, in this case, that is not an exact analogy. The basic idea is pretty simple – you sell the currency pair when you believe or anticipate that the secondary in the currency pair is going to rise in value with respect to the primary. That means that when looking at charts, you are expecting the price to drop. So you are looking to sell when the price is high, and then you'll buy it back when the price is low.

In the case of the EUR/USD pair, if the quote given is 1.20, you might sell the pair if, for some reason, you are expecting the dollar to rise against the Euro. Let's say it drops to 1.10. Then, at that point, you can buy it back. Since you bought it back for a lower price, then you made a profit.

The chart below illustrates the concept.

Some people might get a little confused by selling a currency pair when you sell to open a position. When you sell to open a position, you don't actually own the asset. The way this works is that you borrow the asset from your broker or Forex dealer. This is similar in some respects to shorting a stock.

If you don't know how that works, the basic idea is as follows. To short a stock, you borrow the shares from the broker. Then, you sell them on the open market. For the sake of example, suppose that a given stock was trading at $100 a share. You borrow 10 shares from the broker and sell them for $1,000, expecting the price to decline.

Then, let's say that the price declines to $90 a share. You can then buy the shares back and return them to the broker. Buying them back gives you a profit of $10 a share, for a total profit of $100.

On the Forex market, the concept is basically the same, so you are borrowing the currency pair from the broker and returning it when you buy it back. You don't need to think about this; however, it all happens automatically.

General Idea of Price Movements

The main reason that prices appreciate or depreciate with currency pairs is simple supply and demand. Over the short term, this is mostly driven by speculation among traders. Dramatic news events could also drive supply and demand. You might hear of dollars "fleeing" a certain country or new trade tariffs might make a country seem less attractive to investors, and so Forex traders might want to convert to a different currency. Over the long term, the overall state of the economy is what matters the most. If one economy looks strong relative to another economy, that will make its currency more attractive. That can drive currency traders to invest more in that currency relative to the one they are viewing as weaker.

Whether this news is important or not from your perspective depends on the time frames you use for trading. Many traders use very short or daily time frames. We will talk more about different trading strategies later, but you can generally classify traders like day traders, swing traders, and long-term investors. If you are a day trader, then the macroeconomic news is probably not of interest to you, generally speaking. A day trader will be closely studying the charts looking for signals of short-term price movements. We will talk about how to do this later, but the goal is to look for indicators that show a coming trend reversal. It doesn't matter which direction the trend reversal is going as far as the ability to make profits. If the signals indicate that the trend is going up, then the day trader will buy the currency pair. If the trend is going down, the day trader can sell the currency pair.

Although day trading is a relative term on Forex since there is 24-hours-a-day trading, and it's not constrained in the same way that day trading on the stock markets is, the basic idea is the same. That is, you are looking to enter and exit a position on the same day. In most cases, day trading involves smaller profits on a per-trade basis, but you would be making more frequent trades to make your profit from volume.

Some traders trade on short-term time frames. This is known as scalping. The idea is the same as general day trading, but you are using very short time frames. The scalper is looking to make profits that are very small, but you will trade even more frequently. Since the Forex markets are very volatile, this is what makes scalping something that is possible to do, although it does require the trader to pay close attention to the markets.

So the question is, are day traders exempt from paying attention to the news? Absolutely not. As a day trader, you don't want to get lost in the details. Even though the mechanics of price movements are the bread and butter of the day trader, you need to be aware of the news that hits the airwaves.

A big news event can cause a sudden move in currency prices. It can be economic news, political news, or even something like the breakout of war, even though that hasn't happened lately. Any news that drives fear internationally might drive a sudden shift from one currency to another. The more dramatic the event, the more dramatic the move among currencies might be.

Later we will talk about a strategy called swing trading. This is a more relaxed style of trading, but the goals are basically the same. It's called swing trading because you're looking for price swings for the currency pair. But the difference with day trading is that you're willing to wait for the price swing to occur. You can buy low and sell high, waiting for a day, a few days, or even a few weeks before you sell to exit your position. In some cases, swing traders can even wait a few months. Swing trading is something that requires more patience than day trading if you are unable to sit and wait without being agitated about your investment.

Swing traders need to be paying attention as well, and the longer you hold your trades, the more important macroeconomic news is going to be. The details don't concern us here; the takeaway is that if you expect to be a successful Forex trader, you need to be paying attention to the news in the financial, economic, and political sectors.

Majors

Most currency trading centers around the majors. As you might imagine, since the U.S. dollar is the "reserve currency," it makes up a large fraction of currency trading. The U.S. Dollar is involved in about 89% of currency trades. That doesn't mean you can't make money buying and selling other currency pairs – it's the price movement that determines whether or not you can make a profit. So you should not limit yourself to trades involving the U.S. Dollar. But one factor that is an argument in favor of trading currency pairs involving the U.S. Dollar is that there is more liquidity. The higher trading volume means it's much easier to enter and exit trades. This can be an important factor because when you need to exit a trade, you need to do it ASAP in many circumstances because price reversals can happen fast and wipe out any profits that you've made.

The majors include the U.S. Dollar, the Euro, the Great British Pound, the Australian Dollar, the New Zealand Dollar, The Japanese Yen, and the Canadian Dollar. Oftentimes, these are referred to by traders using nicknames. The U.S. Dollar is called the greenback. The Australian Dollar is called the Aussie, while the New Zealand Dollar is called the Kiwi. The Canadian Dollar goes by the name Looney, and the Great British Pound is sometimes known as the cable. The reasons for those names are historical; the looney refers to a type of bird that used to be on Canadian coins, while the word cable is used because in the early days of currency trading there were underwater cables used to transmit information back and forth between the United States and Great Britain.

PIPs

While you might be used to thinking in terms of dollars, you need to think in new terms on the Forex market, and then convert those terms into dollars. The basic unit of measurement that is used in Forex trading is the percentage in point or PIP. This tells you how the price of a currency pair is shifting.

Currency prices are actually quoted to four or five decimal places. So rather than seeing 1.20 for the Euro and U.S. Dollar, you would read a value like this:

1.2096_2

The fourth number after the decimal place is the PIP. The small number on the end is called the pipette. In many cases, the number is not displayed with a small font, so just count the places after the decimal. The pipette can be ignored for all practical purposes, and it's only been recently added to currency quotes. So, in the above example, the pip is 6, while 2 on end is the pipette.

Just to hammer the point home, let's look at a few more examples. Let's look at the chart and quote below:

AUD to EUR Chart

10 Sep 2019 15:56 UTC **AUD/EUR** close:**0.62168**

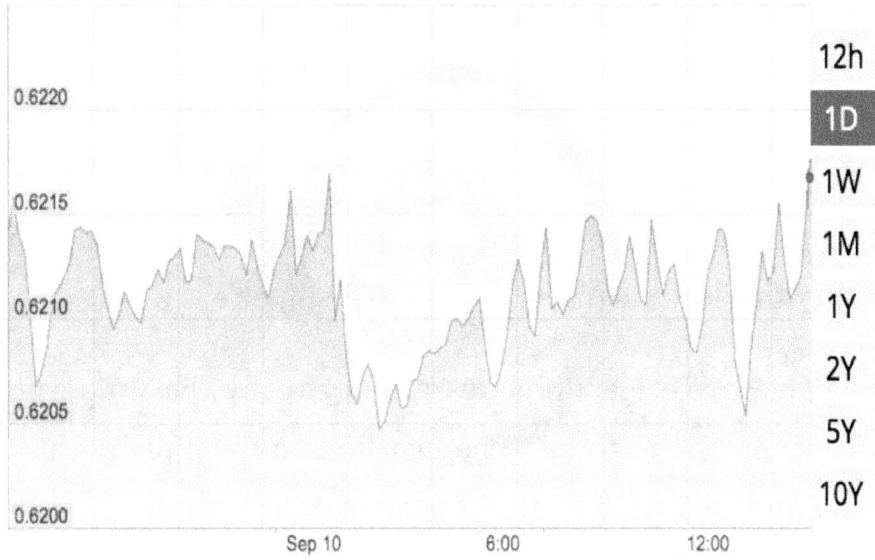

Notice that in this pair, the Australian dollar is the primary, and the Euro is the secondary currency. Again, this really has nothing to do with the values of the currencies, or the size of the economies, or anything like that.

The economy of the European Union is much larger than Australia, and the quote indicates that it takes more Australian dollars to buy Euros. To find out how many Euros you could buy with an Australian dollar, you just invert the value. So you'd need around 1.61 Australian dollars to buy a Euro. As quoted, you'd need 0.62 Euros to buy an Australian dollar.

When you are just starting out, it's always a good idea to review the basic concepts like that. Now, back to the question of the pips. We see the price quoted as:

0.62168

Notice that this website is not listing the pipette in a smaller font. The pip, in this case, is the fourth number after the decimal place, so it's 6. The pipette is 8.

Again, as a trader, pipettes are not really that important. Your interest is going to be focusing on the pips. With that in mind, you need to start focusing on how prices are going up or down in terms of pips.

Let's suppose that you see a price quote for the EUR/USD pair as:

1.35843

In this case, the pip is 4, and the pipette is 3. Later, the price of the EUR/USD is quoted as:

1.35872

Now, the pip is 7, and the pipette is 2. But what we want to focus on is the change. That is the change in pips. If you subtract the numbers, you are going to get 0.00029, but rounding up its 0.0003. So the price went up by 3 pips.

In fact, if you look at different quotes, you are going to see different pipette values, as this example shows for the EUR/USD pair:

EURUSD Forex Chart

FXCM	OANDA	Composite	FOREX.com	Saxo Bank
1.10444	1.10446	1.10430	1.10446	1.10446

Notice that the pipette is often displayed in normal font. As mentioned earlier, getting lost in the pipette isn't worth your time. Just pay attention to the pip, which is the 4th number after the decimal place. As we will see, when looking at some actual examples, the pipette is not influential in terms of actual profits or losses.

If you go from:

1.29031

To:

1.29081

The price went up 5 pips. Now, consider this price quote:

1.40152

If the later price is:

1.40112

Then, the price went down 4 pips. If instead 1.40152 had gone to 1.40262, then the price would have gone up 11 pips. Quotes are not rounded, however, and some brokers will provide quotes without the pipette listed. So, 1.40152 will be listed as 1.4015 by a broker that does not quote the pipette. If the value is 1.40159, the broker is still going to list the quote as 1.4015.

In short, pips are the bread and butter of Forex trading. Now, let's see how this translates into actual practice so that you could use pips to figure out how much money is being gained or lost.

We will again use the example of the Euro and U.S. Dollar currency pair. If the price is quoted as 1.2912, that means that one Euro is worth 1.2912 dollars. Or put another way, 100,000 Euros are worth 129,120 dollars.

This puts pips in terms we can understand for the purposes of making money during Forex trading. If the price changes to 1.2916, that means that now 100,000 Euros are worth 129,160 dollars. This is a move upward of 4 pips. So if you bought 100,000 Euros at the price of 1.2912, then the 4 pip move would mean that you made a profit of 129,160 − 129,120 = $40.

What if the price changed by 20 pips? This would mean that the original price quote of 1.2912 would now be 1.2932. So, 100,000 Euros would be worth 129,320 dollars. Then, the profit would be $129,320 - $129,120 = $200.

The size of the profits depends on a concept that is called lot size. While these numbers might seem crazy at first glance, remember that we can use 50:1 leverage in our trades. And also, remember that as a Forex trader, you are going to be looking at making lots of smaller trades to build up profit over time. The goal is not to make a killing from a single trade when you are a small scale trader.

You can use online calculators to determine the pips and values, rather than trying to do things manually. Just search online for "pip value calculator." However, you should get versed in the differences that pips lead to, and as we will see, it depends on a concept called lot size. And actually, in most cases, you can quickly do the calculations so that you can determine profit or loss.

Japanese Yen

Not all currency pairs have the pip in the fourth decimal place, although that is the situation in most cases. One that you need to be aware of is the Japanese Yen. The pip position, in this case, is going to be the second number after the decimal place. The reason for the difference is that the Japanese Yen is a smaller currency. This is not a reference to the Japanese economy or any inherent value; the Japanese economy is actually one of the largest and most powerful in the world. The way to think about this is to use an analogy in the United States. It would be as if the dime, rather than the dollar, was our standard unit of currency. This is what we mean by "smaller."

So when you see the Japanese Yen in a currency pair, rather than 4 or 5 numbers after the decimal place, you are going to see 2 or 3 numbers after the decimal place. Consider the USD/JPY currency pair. Suppose for the sake of example that the price is quoted as:

110.82

In this case, the pip is 2. It's the second number after the decimal place. If pipettes are included with the Japanese Yen, then it would be listed as something like:

110.827

In this example, the pip is 2, and the pipette is 7.

If you see:

112.74$_1$

Then, you know the pipette is 1, as it's the third decimal place, and it's been made clear for you by using the smaller font. The pip in this example is 4.

The quotes are always displayed in this fashion if the Japanese Yen is one member of the currency pair. So if we see a quote that says:

105.83

And later the same currency pair is quoted as:

105.87

That means the quote increased or went up by 4 pips. If it went from 105.83 to 105.97, then the price would have gone up by 14 pips.

Average PIP Movement

One important metric that you can examine for a given Forex currency pair is called the average PIP movement. This lets you see the average change in pips that the currency pair undergoes over a given time period. You can select the time period to examine, and look at, for example, minute, fifteen minute, hour, day, or month time frames. This will give you an idea of how much prices are changing – on average – in order to get an idea of what kinds of changes in the price you can expect.

Of course, the past is not a guarantee of future behavior, and this is only giving you averages. However, it's a very useful tool to use. The average pip movement can give you an idea of the range of price changes that you can normally expect. Be sure to account for dramatic news that may have occurred over the time period that the average is calculated because, as you know, an outlier can skew average values. The longer the time frame you look at, the more accurate the average pip movement is going to be, generally speaking.

The important thing to take away from the average pip movement is that you can get an estimate for when to enter and exit your positions. It will also give you an idea of what to expect over a given time period. So if the average pip movement for a currency pair over the course of a day is 50 pips, if you are day trading and see an opportunity to buy the currency pair because of a trend reversal after a downturn, you can use this information to estimate you can exit the position after a rise of 40-50 pips in the pricing. On the other hand, if the average for a month is 100 pips, you can use this information for exiting your position as a swing trader.

The average pip movement can be combined with volatility in order to get estimates of future pip movements. For simplicity, suppose that the average daily pip movement is 100 pips for some currency pair. Then, we can look up the volatility in order to estimate the future pip movement. If volatility is high, we can expect larger price movements. Financial advisors often describe volatility as "risky," but in fact, you are often looking for this as a trader. The reason they consider it risky is that they have a long-term investor mentality, and they are focused on potential losses. But as a trader, you are looking to get in and then get out as the price rises. Of course, you have to be aware of sudden price shifts that can happen—but if you are staying on top of things, volatility can actually be your friend.

Spreads

One of the most important concepts to master in the world of Forex trading is the spread. While we've been listing one price for a currency pair, in fact, the prices are given as buying price and selling price. There is going to be a slight difference between the two prices, with a markup price given for the buying price. Price quotes are listed as sell/buy prices, adding a little bit to the confusion. The spread is a markup that the broker or dealer charges—and this is how the Forex dealer does earn their profits. The charge is actually quite small as compared to the kinds of commissions that most stockbrokers charge, but since there are huge numbers of transactions, these charges add up to big money for the Forex dealers.

So, let's say that you see a quote listed as follows:

110.27/110.30

The left side is the selling price. The right side is the buying price, and the markup or spread is the difference between the buying price and the selling price. In this case, it's 0.03.

Sometimes, commissions are charged. Generally speaking, if spreads are tighter, the dealer is going to charge a small commission. Larger spreads can mean small or no commissions.

Now, obviously, you have to figure the cost of spreads and commissions into your trades because it's part of the cost of doing business—and the larger your trades, the higher the fees that you are going to be paying.

When you enter a position in Forex, you are going to be either buying or selling, and then closing the position by selling or buying. So the spread is going to even out at least a little bit. Now, let's say that we see a price quote for the Euro and U.S. Dollar currency pair listed as follows:

1.1820/1.1825

In this case, there is a difference of 0.0005. Remember that the fourth decimal place is a pip. So, if you sell the currency pair, you are starting out down by 5 pips. This is the number that you need to keep in mind, so when you buy the currency pair back, you are looking to make up that 5 pip difference AND profit on top of this.

Remember that if you sell to open a position, you have to buy it back to close the position. Of course, since there is this spread discrepancy, you will, at least, in part, make up the difference of starting a certain number of pips down by making that back when you buy the currency pair.

If you buy to open a trade, then you sell to close the trade. Buying to open gives you a little advantage as far as the spread is concerned.

A rebate occurs if part of the spread is paid back. It's possible to get Forex cashback rebates. When you are making your trades, research this information so that you know how to proceed.

Swaps

At 5 PM eastern time, there is a "rollover" for traders based in the United States. If you carry a trade past this time, the rollover can have an impact. Specifically, there is interest paid or deducted at the rollover. After all, you are holding currency, so it should not come as a surprise that interest is involved. Since interest rates around the world are low, however, this is not going to be a huge factor to consider for most traders, but you do need to be aware of it.

The interest paid at the time of the rollover is called a swap or carry. Depending on the circumstances, the interest can be paid, or it can be deducted. The way this is handled will depend on the interest rate in each country that is a party to the currency pair that you have traded. Let's say we have a hypothetical currency pair:

X/Y

Now, let's say that you buy the currency pair and hold it past the rollover time. If the interest rate of country X is higher than the interest rate of country Y, then you will earn interest. Interest is actually paid out on a minute by minute basis, but of course, interest rates are low, to begin with, and so we are really talking about miniscule amounts. Note that if the interest rate for country Y is higher than the interest rate of country X, then you will actually have to pay interest!

While the amounts are small, if you are someone planning to hold a trade for a long time, in that situation, that might add up. For long periods we are talking weeks to months.

In most cases, the amounts are going to be so small that for all effective purposes, they can be ignored.

You can find an FX Swap Calculator online to calculate the size of a swap or interest payment for a specific currency pair if this is going to be an issue for your particular trades.

Lot Sizes and PIP Values

Now that you have the basic concepts of Forex trading down, it's time to move on and consider lot sizes. Lot sizes are fundamental when it comes to buying and selling on the Forex markets. There are three lot sizes – micro, mini, and standard. In the early days of retail Forex trading, you could only trade standard lot sizes. Since many smaller traders have gotten involved in Forex, lot sizes have been adjusted to give everyone some variety so that smaller traders can trade in lot sizes that are more suitable for the amounts of money that they are able to use in trading.

The lot size is going to determine how many units of currency are involved in a trade. But they are also going to be important in determining the actual value of a PIP. In other words, if you are trading a standard lot size, a 10 pip change does not have the same value as it does when you

86

are trading a mini or a micro lot. So, you want to get an idea of the value of a PIP for different lot sizes so that you can see how man pips a currency pair has moved, and then translate that value into a dollar amount.

Lot sizes are also associated with a concept called volume. That gives you the idea of the size of the trade. Meanwhile, each lot size is ten times larger than the smaller lot size. In other words, a mini lot is 10 times larger than a micro lot, and a standard lot is 10 times larger than a mini lot. And therefore, a standard lot is 100 times larger than the micro lot.

You can also look at this the other way around in terms of fractional values. If the standard lot size is 100 times the size of a micro lot, then that means that a micro lot is 0.01 or 1% the size of a standard lot. A mini lot, therefore, would be 0.10 or 10% the size of a standard lot. The fact that everything is in terms of tens makes it easier to deal with. It is only a matter of actually becoming familiar with the definitions.

So it's the fraction relative to a standard lot—that is what defines the volume. The volume of a standard lot is 1. That means the volume of a micro lot is taken to be 0.01, and the volume of a mini lot is taken to be 0.10.

For a given currency pair, there is a value per pip that is given. These prices are given in our local currency, so for American readers, they will be given in terms of dollars. This helps you to determine the amount of money you earn or lose as the price fluctuates by a given number of pips. When you trade, you are going to want to know your lot size. Then, you are going to want to know the number of pips that it takes to equal a dollar, and then you are going to need to know the number of lots that you traded.

Let's stick with the very popular EUR/USD currency pair. We will start with a micro lot. In this case, 10 pips $1. The volume of a micro lot is 0.01, and we can use this to determine the number of currency units we are trading. This is done by noting that a standard lot is 100,000 currency units. Therefore, a micro lot is:

Micro lot currency units = 0.01 x 100,000 standard lot size = 1,000 currency units

So, if you buy one micro lot of EUR/USD, you are controlling 1,000 Euros. If you sell it, you are controlling $1,000.

Now, we can consider some examples. If you had one micro lot and you sold the micro-lot, and the currency pair quote went up by 5 pips, since 10 pips = $1, that would mean that you made 50 cents. If it went up by 50 pips, you would make $5. All you do is take the number of pips, divide by 10, and then multiply by $1 in order to get the money gained or lost by a price movement. Remember that these values are only for the micro-lot, and specifics may vary at the time of trade or by currency pair.

On the other hand, if you had sold the currency pair in order to open your position, this means that a 5 pip increase in the quote for the currency pair means you lost 5 pips, and with 10 pips to a dollar, that translates into a loss of 50 cents per micro lot.

Now, let's consider the mini lot. A mini lot is ten times the size of a micro lot, and it's a favorite among small retail traders. The volume of a mini lot is 0.1, and as we did above, we can use this information to determine the number of currency units in a trade. In this case:

Mini lot currency units = 0.1 x 100,000 = 10,000

So now we are starting to talk about control of real money. In this case, we are controlling 10,000 units of currency.

That means that if we buy the EUR/USD currency pair, then we are controlling 10,000 Euros. Likewise, if we sell the EUR/USD currency pair, then we are controlling $10,000. The unit is a generic reference to whatever the currency in question is.

For a mini lot, the relation between pips and dollars is scaled up by a factor of ten. That makes sense, right? You are controlling ten times as much currency, and so you are going to be having 10 times as many dollars per pip. Alternatively, since you have ten times as much currency, you are going to see ten times the price movement for a given change in the number of pips.

For a mini lot, you can remember that there is one dollar per pip:

Mini lot: $1 = 1 pip

This is an easy thing to remember, another factor that makes mini lots appealing. So if you buy the currency pair in the form of one mini lot, and it goes up in value by 20 pips, then you've made $20. On the other hand, if it goes down 5 pips, you've lost $5.

Of course, nobody is going to earn a living making $20 a day. So chances are you are going to be trading multiple lots. This concept is easy to understand once it's been explained to you; all that is involved is simple arithmetic. In these examples, we will consider mini lots.

If you were to trade 3 mini lots, to determine your overall profit or loss, just multiply the basic relationship by 3. The basic relationship for a mini lot is just $1 = 1 pip. So if you trade 3 lots, then the relationship becomes $3 = 1 pip. That should be pretty simple to understand, because a pip causes a one-dollar price movement in a single lot, so you have three lots, and a one pip movement is going to cause a total or net price movement of $3 for your 3 lots.

If you trade 5 mini lots, then the value per pip is going to be $5. If you trade 7 lots, then it's going to be $7 per pip and so on.

To determine the same relationship using micro-lots, start with the basic relationship that it takes 10 pips to equal one dollar. Looked at in a more productive or useful way, this means that 1 pip is 10 cents. So, if you trade 2 micro lots, the relationship for the trade becomes 1 pip is 20 cents. If you were to trade 7 micro lots, then 1 pip is 70 cents.

Now, let's use this information with a few exercises to get more practice. For the first example, suppose that you are trading with mini lots, and you have bought 12 lots of the EUR/USD pair. The basic relationship is then going to be the value per pip is $12.

So what happens if the quote for the EUR/USD currency pair goes up by 38 pips? In this case – since you bought the currency pair, a rise in the number of pips means that you've made money. The specific amount would be:

$12/pip x 38 pips = $456

Of course, there is a more fundamental way to write this down:

$1/pip x # of mini lots x # pips

Now, suppose that you traded 7 mini lots, and the price went up by 57 pips. Then, you would have gained:

$1/pip x 7 lots x 57 pips = $399

Of course, you can lose money too. Let's use a micro lot example to illustrate this situation. Remember that for a micro lot, there is $0.10 per pip. If you were to trade 5 lots (buying the currency pair) and the quote for the EUR/USD currency pair dropped by 23 pips, then you would lose:

$0.10/pip x 5 lots x 23 pips = $11.50

The situations are reversed if you are selling a currency pair. In that case, you actually want the quote of the currency pair to drop, as you are actually betting on the secondary in the currency pair. For the case of the EUR/USD, if you sell the currency pair you are betting that the U.S. dollar is going to rise against the Euro in value, which will mean that the quote given – that represents the number of dollars you can buy with one Euro – will drop if it is to move in your favor.

So, if you were to sell 25 mini lots and the EUR/USD dropped by 75 pips, you would make:

$1/pip x 25 mini lots x 75 pips/lot = $1,875

Now that would be a pretty decent profit. On the other hand, consider this example. Again, say you sell the EUR/USD currency pair. This time you sell 8 mini lots. But let's say that the quote actually rises by 150 pips. That means that you would be losing money. How much money? It would be:

$1/pip x 8 mini lots x 150 pips/lot = $1,200

We hate to cause pain during reading; after all, you are probably reading this book, hoping to get excited about Forex trading! And you should – but you have to be realistic and understand what different values can mean for you in terms of losses, not just gains. We don't want to be immature and only imagine ourselves winning on every trade. It doesn't work out that way for anyone, even if you are a major currency trader like George Soros himself.

Now, let's move up and consider standard lot sizes. Most new traders are not going to be trading in standard lot sizes, and even if you have the money required to do so, you should avoid trading standard lot sizes when starting out. When you are talking about trading standard lot sizes, we are beginning to talk about serious money, and when you are learning the tools of the "trade," you don't want to take unnecessary and unwarranted risks. When it comes to trading, patience and care are virtues.

Let yourself become experienced in the market and with trading rather than thinking in terms of hitting one or two big trades. Also, remember that old maxim that you can save a million dollars a penny at a time. The same holds true with Forex trading; you can earn a million dollars one mini lot at a time.

But you need to be familiar with standard lot sizes, even if you end up never actually trading standard lot sizes. When the Forex markets first became open to the general public, there were only standard lot sizes available. This somewhat limited the markets because of the larger amounts of money that were necessary in order to get in the game.

A standard lot size is 100,000 units of currency. So that means if you are trading a standard lot of a currency pair that includes the U.S. Dollar, you are controlling $100,000 worth of that currency.

That is a concept worth reviewing. Let's go over this using all of the lot sizes:

- If you are trading a standard lot of EUR/USD, you are controlling $100,000 worth of Euros.

- If you are trading a micro lot of EUR/USD, you are controlling $1,000 worth of Euros.

- If you are trading a mini lot of USD/JPY, you are controlling $10,000 worth of Japanese Yen.

- If you are trading five micro-lots of AUD/USD, you are controlling $1,000 worth of Australian dollars per lot, for a total of $5,000.

- If you are trading 3 standard lots of GBP/USD, you are controlling $100,000 worth of GBP per lot, for a total of $300,000.

Of course, you are actually controlling the currency pair, which you buy or sell to bet on which currency you think is going to appreciate in value relative to the other one.

Now, getting back to a standard lot, it's the reference point for the other lot sizes. That means the volume of a standard lot is unity, or we can put it this way – the volume of a standard lot is:

Volume = 1.0

So, the trade size is one lot. Using the relationships that we discussed earlier, a single mini lot means that the trade size is 0.10 lots, and a single micro-lot means that the trade size would be 0.01 lots.

It might be tedious going through these things over and over but getting used to it means that you will be able to understand trading on the Forex markets – so it's worth going through.

Since there is $1 per pip for a mini lot, and a standard lot is ten times the size, that means the value per pip is $10 for a standard lot. If the quote goes up by 30 pips, that means you've made $300.

Oftentimes, traders will often speak in terms of how many pips you made or lost. We can familiarize ourselves with this lingo as well by doing some more simple exercises with standard lot sizes.

If a trader says they made 50 pips on the trade of 3 standard lots, they made:

50 pips x $10/pip x 3 standard lots = $1,500

If the trader lost 30 pips on the trade of 5 standard lots, the total loss in terms of dollars would be:

30 pips x $10/pip x 5 standard lots = $1,500

Again, the fact that lots, in values of 10, makes doing the calculations rather easy.

Trade Sizes

Now, let's make sure that all readers are comfortable with the notions of trade size. You need to understand whether a trade is micro, mini, or standard based on the dollar amounts of the trade. Here, we are going to define account sizes based on the lots that we looked at in the previous section. The general definitions are as follows:

- $1,000 or less – this is a micro account.

- $5,000 - $10,000 – this is a mini account.

- $100,000 – standard account.

An important issue that you will face as a Forex trader is how much cash you need in your account in order to trade a given number of lots, as well as how much risk you are willing to accept. We will discuss these issues in chapter 8 when we talk about trading plans.

Chapter 5: Majors and Exotics

In this chapter, we are briefly going to discuss the different currency pairs that exist. You can trade the majors, which is what most people are going to be doing—but you can also trade lesser-known and less popular currency pairs. Some of these are known as "exotics." There are advantages and disadvantages to doing so; for example, one issue that should always concern you is the liquidity of a given trading pair. If you are trading the mystery island peso against the secret hilltop dollar, when you need to close your position to exit a trade, it might be hard to find someone to take the other side of the trade in order to close it out. Of course, there is always the possibility of having the dealer take the other end of the trade, but first, let's take a look at the majors.

The Major Currency Pairs

The U.S. Dollar is involved in some 89% of currency trades, and currency pairs that involved the U.S. Dollar and some other currency from a large, developed economy are called the majors. There are seven major currency pairs. Let's take a look at each one so that you will be familiar with what people are talking about when they mention the majors. A major currency pair can be any of the following.

EUR/USD

The Euro and U.S. Dollar currency pair is the most popular and widely traded of the majors. The Euro was introduced in 1999, and it's a relatively strong currency that represents all the major countries in Europe that are part of the European Union. Although Brexit is dominating recent headlines, even with Britain as a part of the European Union, it has maintained its own currency, the Great British Pound. Hence, the Euro is the currency used by members of the EU on the continent.

When it comes to this currency pair, you are going to want to watch moves by the European Central Bank or ECB, and also the U.S. Federal Reserve. Of course, in any of the majors, you are going to be looking at moves by the U.S. Federal Reserve.

The biggest strength of this currency pair from the perspective of a small retail trader is that it is a highly liquid financial asset that often has substantial volatility. In recent years, the volatility and the magnitude of moves (on average) have decreased somewhat, but it's still a rather strong average pip movement of 200 pips. Since this currency pair is so liquid, getting in and out of trades fast is not going to be an issue. This currency pair is certainly a good choice for beginners, or for a trader of any level.

USD/JPY

This is the U.S. Dollar and Japanese Yen currency pair. Japan isn't quite the monolith that it was in the 1980s when everyone thought that Japan would take over the entire world economically, but Japan still maintains a large and powerful economy dominated by well-known companies like Toyota, Subaru, and Sony, among others. One factor that is important when considering this currency pair is the fact that Japan remains one of the world's largest exporting nations. This means that it's a frequently traded and highly liquid currency because all that exporting means that people have to convert dollars into Yens and vice versa all the time. The interest rate is low, which also makes this currency pair more attractive for holding over longer time periods.

GBP/USD

As we mentioned above, despite being a long-time member of the European Union, Great Britain held onto its own currency rather than adopt the Euro in 1999. Now that Britain may exit the European Union, for good or for worse, this probably means that the Great British Pound is here to stay for the foreseeable future. We noted earlier in the book that this was once (and sometimes still is) referred to as the cable, as currency trading between the United States and Great Britain went on via electronic cable under the Atlantic Ocean starting in the late 19th century.

Brexit may introduce a lot of volatility in this currency pair, and in fact, in any currency pair involving GBP, and so traders may want to pay attention to it at least for the near future. Even after Brexit is finalized, if it ever actually is, then there is likely to be some extra volatility introduced into the price movements of GBP currency pairs. Whether that is in favor of the GBP or against it, that is not a question that is relevant to the Forex trader. You are not favoring one currency over another because you like it, you are picking currencies based on what works in a given trade.

USD/CHF

CHF is the ticker symbol (to use a stock analogy) for the Swiss Franc. Switzerland is another country maintaining its own currency, and given Switzerland's strong banking presence, it's an important currency despite the relatively small size of the country and its economy. Traders consider the Swiss Franc to be an important currency during times of economic trouble, or when there is an international crisis. When there are international problems, in most cases, the Swiss Franc can be expected to increase against the U.S. Dollar because the demand for the Franc rises as people look for a relatively safe place to put their money.

So, if there is an economic crisis that you happen to experience, remember this and bet on the Swiss Franc against the dollar. In times of uncertainty, economic downturn, or crisis, the Swiss Franc may also do well against several other currencies such as the Japanese Yen. The USD/CHF pair sometimes goes by the nickname, "Swissie."

USD/CAD

Although Canada has a relatively small population compared to the European Union, Japan, and the United States, its economy enjoys outsized importance because it shares a border with the United States, and a large amount of trade goes on between the two countries. Canada has a lot of natural resources that it exports, such as oil, natural gas, and timber, which again helps it to maintain an outsized level of importance in the world of economics and in currency trading. Due to its direct relationship with the United States, the USD/CAD currency pair can be a good trade, even though it doesn't play as large a role in the markets as the EUR/USD currency pair does. When relations between Canada and the United States are good, volatility can decrease for this currency pair.

When there are some difficulties, this can lead to increased volatility making it more attractive to trade. Canada has large exports of coal, raw aluminum, iron ore, gold, and copper ore. So to get a feel for how the movement of the Canadian dollar may be trending with respect to other currencies, you might want to see if the prices of these commodities are rising or falling. Since Canada is exporting these materials, this generally means that rising commodity prices are good for Canadian currency.

AUD/USD

Australia is a diverse and highly modern economy, but like Canada, it's economic fortunes are often influenced very heavily by the export of natural resources. When it comes to Australia, you will want to pay attention to iron ore and rare earth metals, along with coal. When commodity prices are rising, the fortunes of Australia are often rising with it, but when they are declining, the fortunes of Australia are probably going down as well. When you are trading any currency pair involving the Australian dollar, you will want to look at the prices of various commodities, but especially coal and iron ore, to see how they are going. Australia also exports large amounts of gold, petroleum, and wheat. So favorable pricing moves for these commodities may put the Australian dollar in a position to rise against other currencies.

NZD/USD

The last of the majors is the currency pair between the New Zealand Dollar and the U.S. Dollar. The New Zealand economy isn't as large as the others we've considered, and it's highly dependent on tourism and the export of agricultural products. It is a leading exporter of dairy products as well as lamb and other meats. If dairy prices are rising on commodities markets, this can bode well for any currency pair involving the NZD.

Crosses

If the USD is not in the currency pair, these are called crosses. There are crosses for each of the currencies from major economies, such as the Euro or the Japanese Yen. The majors enjoy the highest trading volume and are therefore the most liquid currency pairs that you can trade, but there are several crosses that also have high trading volume, and so can be good to trade as well.

First, let's look at some of the Euro crosses.

- EUR/JPY: As you might imagine, there is a lot of trade that goes on between these two major economies. As a result, this can be a good currency pair to trade. When exports are in favor, Japan might have an edge, in particular when electronic components are considered.

- EUR/CHF: This is the Euro and Swiss Franc cross pair. The thing to look for here is the overall economic situation and whether there are any international tensions. Generally speaking, if people are looking for a safe refuge for their money, the Swiss Franc is going to be it. So when times are tough, you might look for increased volatility with this currency pair, and you might also look for the Swiss Franc to be rising in value against the Euro.

- EUR/GBP: This is certainly a currency pair to watch with the pending Brexit move, no matter how it turns out. If the situation is viewed favorably in terms of the European Union, then certainly, the Euro is going to rise in value against the Great British Pound. In the near future, at least, the Great British Pound is probably going to be declining in value against several major currencies, although over time, this will probably stabilize, and once things settle down, the Great British Pound is probably going to be rising in value. But for now, look for it to be the weaker member of a currency pair with another major country.

- AUD: The Australian dollar is also a good cross to look at when trading with the Japanese Yen, New Zealand Dollar, Euro, Canadian Dollar, and even against the Chinese Yuan. The main thing to look at when it comes to the Australian Dollar is to look at what Australia exports and who is importing from it. When commodity prices are rising, this is something that is going to favor the Australian Dollar against the currencies of those countries that are importing large amounts of raw materials from Australia. China is a big consideration here.

- Japanese Yen: Any cross pair involving JPY is going to be important. The key data point for Japan is to remember that Japan has few (if any) natural resources, but it's going to be importing a large number of commodities since it has a thriving export business of major manufactured goods like automobiles. Therefore, rising commodity prices may be something that hurts Japanese currency, while falling commodity prices might help it, as that means the steel in Toyotas and Nissan cars are going to cost Japanese companies less, and lead to increased sales worldwide.

Exotic Currency Pairs

Exotic currency pairs are generally going to include currencies from countries that we have not yet discussed. These are currencies that are not traded nearly as much, but many exotic currencies are going to be associated with developing countries. Examples can include countries like Mexico, Thailand, and Brazil. Some currencies that fall in the exotic category have manipulated or fixed exchange rates, making trading them problematic. The biggest weakness with exotic currencies is that they tend to have small trading volumes. Professional Forex traders are generally not spending their time focusing on exotic currency pairs.

Some exotics like the Mexican Peso are more stable than others, such as the Iraqi dinar. But the biggest weakness for any exotic currency is that they are not highly desired by traders, and as a result, you might find yourself stuck in trade far longer than you want to be.

The economies of many exotic currencies are also unstable and subject to more political upheaval than the economies of most major countries. This means that volatility can suddenly be sent soaring on some political event. Rapid depreciation can often be seen with exotic currencies, and while this can offer an opportunity to bet against the currency, remember that getting out of a trade is something that can always be an issue. So there are two main weaknesses that you need to consider when thinking about trading exotics – instability and low levels of liquidity.

However, there are some reasons that traders will find trading exotic currency pairs to be worth their while. The first is that they move a lot. If you put the time in to study the charts of exotic currency pairs, you are going to find that they can move by large amounts, and then the price movement will come to a grinding halt. The movements can be extremely large – even on the order of thousands of pips, making it possible for traders to get large profits if they are able to get in the trade and the right time, and they are able to sell their position before the price goes down again.

One factor that influences exotic currency pairs is that they are only traded by a relatively small number of banks, whereas the U.S. Dollar is going to be traded by all banks. So this is something that can work for or against you. When there is a price movement of the exotic currency pair, it's going to be quite large. Since there are not large numbers of institutions or traders (relatively speaking) trading the exotic currency pair, this means that it's not easy to reverse a trend in price that happens when banks make their moves on these currency pairs. If you are following a trend trading strategy (see future chapter), then exotic currency pairs might be something to look into. But again, the biggest problem with exotic currency pairs is that at some point you need to get out of the trade – and it might be difficult to find someone to take the opposite side of the trade so that you can close out your position.

One exception to the rule might be exotic currencies that are paired with the U.S. Dollar. For example, one of the favorites in this regard is the U.S. Dollar and the Mexican Peso. The United States and Mexico are involved in a significant amount of trade, and so this currency pair is going to have more liquidity than many other exotics. However, it's a currency pair that is often going to have large moves in price, which can either be sudden moves that can result in large profits or solid trending. Either way, it's an exotic currency pair that is a middle ground because of the large amount of trade between the two countries coupled with the fact that people are always looking for U.S. Dollars in countries with developing economies, because their currency is not as stable and trustworthy, while the dollar, for all its faults, fills these roles. So there may be exotic currencies that could be worth trading, but you need to do some research before just jumping in.

Summary: Currency Pairs

Most traders are better off sticking with the major currency pairs, at least until you build up a large amount of experience. Because of the large amount of liquidity that is accessible to traders of the majors, you can use a larger variety of trading strategies, and something you never have to worry about is getting in and out of trades quickly.

Chapter 6: Trading Strategies

Now, you should have a good idea of what Forex trading is, the basic concepts used, and what the currency pairs are all about and how to identify them. In this chapter, we are going to review trading strategies and techniques. There are many different approaches to trading that can be used, and you really can't say whether one is better than another, or whether you will make a profit using one technique over another. The overall strategy that you select for your own trading activities is going to be a matter of taste.

Demo Accounts

If you are just starting out with Forex trading—especially if you are a beginning trader overall, not even having experience on the stock market or with trading options—then you should consider spending a few days or week with a demo account before entering a real trade. The demo accounts available today are very sophisticated, and they work exactly like a real account would so you can get a feel for placing and making trades—and seeing how they work out. The Meta Trader platform has an MT5 app that you can download to your phone and use to make practice trades. This is highly recommended for new traders, especially if you are going to be getting involved with fast, high-pressure trading like scalping or day trading.

Carry Trading

One of the strategies that are used is called a carry trade. In simple terms, you look to sell currency from a country that has a lower interest rate than the currency it is trading against. This is something that can lead to profits. In today's low-interest-rate environment, this can be hard to find, but one recent example that is used to illustrate the strategy is the Australian Dollar against the Japanese Yen. At the time, this was good for this currency pair; the Australian interest rate was nearly 6 points higher than the interest rate in Japan.

This is an unusually large interest rate differential, but it serves to illustrate the point. The currency pair in question is AUD/JPY – so you are actually buying the currency pair in this case. That is, if the secondary has a lower interest rate, you want to buy the currency pair. If the primary has a lower interest rate, then you want to sell the currency pair. In this case, since Australia had a higher interest rate, demand for the currency was higher than demand for the Japanese Yen when it came to this particular currency pair, and so while the condition existed, the price kept trending upward over a long time period.

Scalping

Scalping is a popular Forex strategy that requires a full-time devotion to following the Forex markets. The idea behind scalping is to earn small profits on trades that involve small movements up and down, and then you earn a living by doing a large number of trades. This is a highly involved strategy that requires you to be constantly paying attention to the market. For the most part, fundamental analysis is not going to be used, unless there is some dramatic event that you can take advantage of right at the moment. And in fact, scalpers often seek to take advantage of large price moves that occur when important news is released. This can include news about changes in interest rates, unemployment, GDP numbers, or even unexpected news such as a dramatic or important political event or international incident.

The analysis used for scalping has to be done in real-time. The goal is to make small profits on each trade, 10 pips here, 5 pips there, maybe 15 pips over here. Positions are held for a very short time. If you buy a currency pair and it rises by a few pips (remember, it has to be enough to cover any spread as well), then you sell the currency pair and take the small level of profits. Then, you are going to enter another trade and repeat the process all day long. Since the profit level is going to be small for each trade, the scalper must do a large number of trades in order to make a living each day.

Scalping is often compared to day trading. However, scalping is actually quite a bit more involved than day trading is. So if you find that day trading is not your style, you are unlikely to find scalping very appealing. A day trader may only enter into one or two positions on any given trading day. A scalper will enter far more positions. The day trader will exit positions that same trading day; the scalper may be exiting positions over the course of minutes.

Scalpers are looking to make profits on the order of as little as 5 pips per trade, and then up to 10 pips per trade. Then, they keep making trades all day long. Since Forex trades 24 hours, you can scalp as long as you want to.

If you are scalping using micro-lots, it will take a very large number of trades to start making decent money. However, if you are trading standard lots, it's possible to make good money on a reasonable number of trades. For a standard lot, recall that one pip is $10. So a 10 pip move on a standard lot is $100. Even a mere 5 pip move would mean $50 in profit. That may not sound like much, but if you were able to get three 10 pip trades and five 5 pip trades, that would amount to $550 in income for the day. Of course, whether or not you actually get winning trades day-in and day-out is another issue. It's something that takes a special skill and the ability to focus, and a thorough knowledge of technical analysis.

A scalper has to be someone who does not hesitate or overanalyze. If you are the kind of person who might hesitate while under pressure, you might not be suited for scalping. You have to be able to act in the heat of the moment, with money on the line. So if you see a trade losing money, then you will need to be able to act quickly to cut your losses. Many people find this difficult because they start going over "what if" scenarios in their minds.

As a scalper, that kind of thinking not only doesn't have any place, it's not even important. The reason it's not important is that you are going to be getting in on multiple trades throughout the day, and so worrying about a single trade going bad it not going to be worth your energy.

One thing that is important if you decide to use scalping as your strategy is you have to pay close attention to the spread. You will remember that the spread is going to be a fee that you pay when trading on Forex. Many traders are not very worried about the spread because they are looking for higher levels of profit on their trades, which will be larger in magnitude than the spread. In contrast, the scalper is looking just to make a profit of 5 or 10 pips – and so the spread can really cut into the potential profits that a scalper can make.

A spread might be one, two, or three pips. So you see that if you are looking to make a five pip profit, the spread is going to be impactful. If it was, say, two pips, then you are going to have to actually see a price movement of seven pips in order to make a profit. So if you are a scalper, you have to let the market move to cover the spread before you have a chance to make profits.

Using Leverage as Part of Your Strategy

Leverage – at the high levels available on the Forex markets – is one of the factors that has made Forex trading one of the most popular ways to trade. As we mentioned earlier, while a stock trader can only access 2:1 leverage, a Forex trader can access leverage at 50:1 in the United States and even much higher in other countries. In short, this means that you are borrowing money in order to make trades. The money is borrowed from the broker. In order to use leverage, you have to have a margin, which just means a certain amount of cash in your account.

The margin requirement is often expressed as a percentage. It could be 1% or 2%; it will depend on your broker and where you are located. In the U.S., it's usually going to be a 2% requirement. All you have to do in order to figure out the amount of capital required to trade a certain amount is to multiply that by the margin requirement. So, in order to trade 2 standard lots, which is 100,000 currency units, you would need 2% * 100,000 = $2,000 per lot. So if you had $4,000 cash, you could trade two standard lots of 100,000 units of currency each. The leverage is then calculated by taking the standard lot size and dividing it by the required deposit – so 100,000/2,000 = 50. This is how we get the 50:1 leverage allowed in the United States. In other words, you need 2% down to borrow the rest of the money.

To figure out how much you can trade, just divide the amount of money by 2%.

If you have an account with $500, then you can trade up to $25,000. So you could trade to mini lots and then trade five micro-lots. If you only had $100, you could still trade $5,000 worth or five micro-lots. Check with your broker to determine what they actually allow.

Day Trading

One of the more popular strategies is day trading. If you are a day trader on the Forex markets, all that means is that you buy and sell currency pairs on the same trading day. You may decide to sell before 5 PM so that you can avoid getting tangled up in the interest rate (swaps) issue. The goal behind day trading is somewhat similar to that used by scalpers. Basically, you will use leverage to enter positions. You might do a small number of positions as compared to a scalper, perhaps two to three per day. Since you are trading a smaller number of positions, you are going to be looking to make higher levels of profit per trade. So a 5 pip move, while that might cut it for a scalper, it is probably not going to work for a day trader.

Day traders and scalpers will tend to focus on the major currency pairs. The reason is liquidity. That is important for both trading styles. What the liquidity does is that it ensures the day trader or scalper can immediately get out of a position when they have to. Many people trading on Forex recommend trading the EUR/USD pair. Not only is it very liquid, but it's also a currency pair that fluctuates by large amounts over short time periods. In other words, it's a highly volatile currency pair, and the price fluctuations of the EUR/USD currency pair are going to make it very favorable when you are seeking out the kind of price movements that can lead to profits over short time periods.

In order to day trade Forex, your broker may have a capital requirement, but they may not. Forex trading is not regulated to the extent that stock trading is regulated. Therefore, you will need to check with different brokers in order to find out what the specific requirements are.

Day traders, like scalpers, are going to rely heavily on technical analysis. However, just like a scalper, a day trader needs to be staying on top of the news. Big news events can cause large movements in price that will lead to large profits (or losses if they move against you), and so day traders need to be paying close attention so that they don't get caught by surprise or miss potential opportunities.

Day traders will study candlestick charts, probably on five-minute or 15-minute time intervals. They are also going to use moving averages, and possibly the relative strength indicator.

Breakout Day Trading

In fact, scalping is really a subset of day trading. The other type of day trading that is followed is called breakout trading. With breakout trading, you are looking to earn profits on a large trend reversal. This can be done on a simple technical basis, so you would be watching the computer to find signals in the data of a coming trend reversal. You are probably going to be using multiple indicators, and so you are going to wait for them to all agree a price reversal is coming, and so you can enter your position. A day trader can enter a position as a buyer or seller. This is done in the standard way, so if you are a buyer, you are looking for the price of the currency pair to increase after a downtrend. If you are a seller, you will look for an uptrend running out of steam, to be replaced by a downward trend in price, so that you can buy back the currency pair at a lower value, and earn profits.

Besides looking for data coming out of the charts and technical indicators, a day trader is going to be keeping an eye on the news, looking for events that might lead to a breakout. This can be any news that will have a positive or negative impact on some currency. The news can be unexpected, so you have to keep an eye on the news while you are doing everything else. Many times, you can trade on expected news, such as a federal reserve interest rate cut, or the announcement of GDP growth rates.

If the news is going to be good for the U.S. dollar, you can sell the EUR/USD currency pair and then earn profits when the price of the currency pair drops because the demand for the dollar is rising. Conversely, if the news was bad for the dollar, then you could buy the currency pair, and wait for it to rise in the expected price direction to a point where you can take profits.

Swing Trading

The next trading strategy we are going to look at is called swing trading. Any financial market goes through price swings, which are simply ups and downs in prices. An example is shown in this chart here:

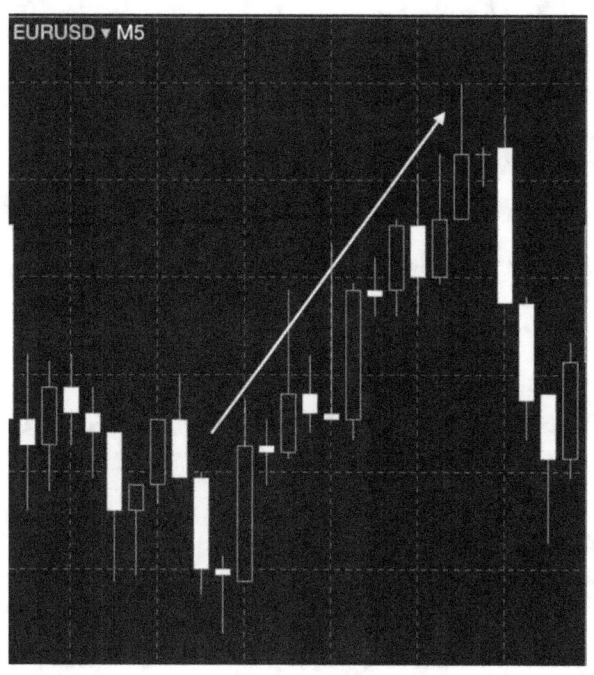

A price swing is an opportunity to make a profit. Of course, it's not something that is automatic, but the idea is to enter a position at the right moment, as a new price swing is developing. Then, you would exit the position when the price swing is coming to an end and about to reverse. If you are buying a currency pair, you will buy when you believe the price has reached a minimum value for the time period of interest, and then hold the position until it reaches an anticipated maximum. There are ways to estimate what these minimums and maximums are, and swing traders also use the technical indicators and candlestick charts day traders use to anticipate trend reversals.

You can also use downward swings in a currency pair chart to profit by selling the currency pair. It's the same idea, but in reverse – you sell the currency pair at the peak when there are signs of a coming downward trend. Then, you buy it back when the price has dropped to a level you are satisfied with.

While day trading is a trading strategy that incorporates the idea of exiting your positions on the same trading day, swing trading is a longer-term strategy. There are no set rules on how long-term you can make it, but swing traders will hold their positions at least overnight. Some swing traders will hold their positions for a few days or even a few weeks. It's possible also to hold positions for several weeks. Remember that if you hold your positions for an extended time period like this, swaps (interest) could be an issue to consider.

Since swing traders hold positions for extended time periods, this is a preferred method of trading for those who are trading on a part-time basis. If you are day trading, whether you are scalping or using breakout trading strategies, it is going to require you to be paying full-time attention to the markets, sitting at your computer staring at charts, looking for the right moment to enter and exit a trade.

If you are looking for a price swing over the course of a few days to weeks, you still have to look for the best time to enter the position, but you don't have to watch it constantly. You will simply wait for the price to move where you want it to be, and therefore you are only checking it periodically since you're looking for slower price movements. In fact, after placing your trade, you might not have to check it at all. As we will see in the next chapter, you can use risk mitigating methods to make your exits automatic.

Swing trading is essentially the best of both worlds. It uses the technical analysis and profit-seeking methods of day trading, but over a longer time scale, which reduces the pressure on the trader. However, it can require more patience. If you have a more anxious disposition and you want to see fast results, you might prefer day trading, rather than waiting days or weeks to see if your trade is going to work out. Ask yourself if you are going to be able to sleep at night, night after night, knowing that your money is tied up in a trade. If the answer is no, then you might look at day trading rather than using swing trading. But if you are able to maintain your cool following this type of strategy, and you are even able to wait weeks to see the trade either work out or fail, then swing trading might be a strategy that is suitable for you.

When you are swing trading, you are going to enter larger trades than you would day trading. Generally speaking, a swing trader is going to enter fewer trades, but hope to make more profits per trade. This is another difference that will play a role in determining which trading style is best for your situation. Some people would rather do multiple small trades over short time periods, while others would prefer to focus their attention on a small number of trades and have more riding on each trade.

Even within the realm of swing trading, there can be a lot of variation. You might be doing more frequent trading, say looking for profits over a day or a few days at the most, or you might have fewer trades, with each trade lasting weeks at a time. Swing trading is a pretty flexible trading strategy, and so you can take either approach.

Swing trading works with two basic types of price swings. The main one people are looking for is a large price swing. So you are hoping to get in on a short-term trend that can either take the price of a currency pair much higher and so you buy the pair or take it from a peak down to a new low. You would sell the pair in that case.

Often, however, prices are trapped within a range. This phenomenon is called ranging, and what happens, in this case, is the price will bounce up and down in between two pricing levels. The low pricing level is called support because it ensures that the asset never drops below. In order to have support, traders look for the price to touch the support line at least two times over a given time range and remember the price would not dip below the support level.

At the top end of the range, there would be a high price that the asset cannot break above. This pricing level is called resistance. Again, the asset price would reach the resistance price, or close to it, at least two times over the time period of interest, and it would never break above it.

Ranging is an opportunity to make smaller profits. First, let's consider buying a currency pair. You wait until the price drops to the support level, then you buy the currency pair. Now, it's only a matter of waiting – you wait until the price rises to the resistance level, and then sell to exit the position.

Alternatively, if you are selling the currency pair, you can sell it when the price is at the relative high point, at or near the resistance level. Then, you simply wait for the price to drop down to the support level, and you buy back the currency pair.

Ranging is going to result in smaller profits per trade, but it's a way to earn money when the currency pair is not breaking high or low. Of course, your trade can go bad because something may happen, leading the currency pair out of the ranging pattern with a breakout. Financial assets can stay in a ranging pattern for an extended time period, but they can also break out of them and will break out of them at some point.

Swing trading will involve using both technical analysis and fundamental analysis. The longer that you hold your position, the more that fundamental analysis becomes important. This will be true for both random events and regular timed announcements. If you hold your positions for longer time periods, technical analysis will be less important.

Position Trading

The idea of swing trading can be extended out for even longer time periods. This trading style is known as position trading, where you can hold a position for a minimum of several months to a year. In fact, some position traders will hold their trades for several years.

Position trading is going to be based far more on fundamental analysis than technical analysis. The longer-term trends of currency pairs are impacted by the economic data in each country. Technical analysis can be said to be irrelevant to the position trader. Instead of pouring over charts looking for signals of price reversals, you are going to be studying the fundamentals of each economy, including interest rates, unemployment numbers, GDP numbers, trade, and so forth. Your interest isn't even going to be focused on a specific release of information; instead, you are going to be looking at long-term outlooks. So you might be anticipating a period of a year or two of growing GDP, for example.

Forex markets are very volatile, and so a position trader will have to be prepared for large price swings. The trades have to be set up properly in order to manage the possibilities of a price moving up or down in such a manner that it could lead to a margin call.

The main virtues of position traders are extreme patience, and a willingness to study long-term economic data while drawing the correct conclusions about the trends in the economy. Of course, you are going to have to rely on the opinions of experts while doing this, in addition to making your own judgments about coming trends.

Position traders tend to have larger accounts. More capital will be needed to cover potential losses. In addition, you are going to be making fewer trades, with more money riding on each trade. Position trading can involve managing swings of hundreds of pips while waiting for the trend to move in your direction, over the time period that you intend to hold the position.

As a position trader, you will have to educate yourself on fundamental analysis. This will require a solid understanding of macroeconomics, money, and banking. You are going to have to understand how macroeconomic changes and interest rate changes impact currency pairs.

A position trader may be looking to earn several hundred to several thousand pips per trade. So they are not going to be looking at exiting a trade with smaller price movements. This is a calm and deliberate style of trading. If you are not able to enter a trade with a large amount of capital on the line for a single trade and wait months for it to materialize while ignoring gains of 20, 50, or 100 pips, then you are probably not suited for position trading. If you are not interested in macroeconomic forces, position trading might not be your style because the bottom line is you must do a lot of fundamental analysis to be a position trader.

But if you are patient, and willing to ride out massive price swings while waiting for large gains, position trading could be your style.

Trend Trading

Often, a financial asset will enter a long-term trend up or down in price. A common practice among traders is to trade with the trend. You can trade with the trend no matter what overall strategy you are using, and trends can occur over multiple time frames. Trading with the trend is pretty simple—you enter a position at the start of the trend and then exit your position when you've made desired profits.

The chart below illustrates a downward trend, which would be an opportunity to profit from the secondary member of the currency pair.

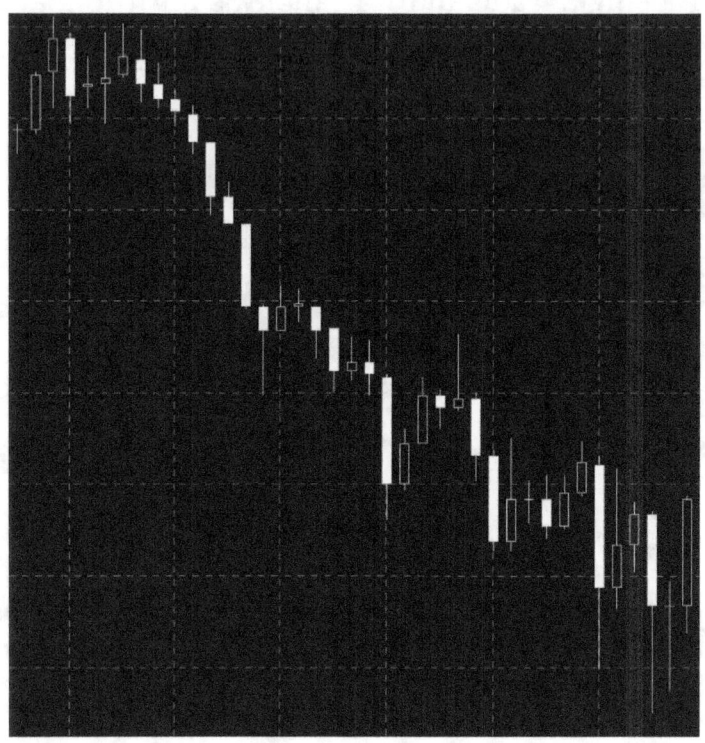

Trading Full-Time or Part-Time

The amount of time that you can or want to devote to trading is going to have some impact on the strategies and trading style that you can use. The main thing to keep in mind is that day trading (including scalping) is an activity that will require a full-time devotion to the markets. Of course, you can do this at night if you are able, but doing it during the day while trying to maintain a full-time job may not be something that is feasible for most people. You can work your way into this if that is your goal, however.

Start by swing trading, and you can learn how to use technical indicators and get some experience engaging in trades. Swing trading is something that can be done on a part-time basis. For some, they are going to want to stick to trading part-time. However, others might use a few months of swing trading to start building up an income and transitioning into day trading on a full-time basis.

You can do scalping on a part-time basis as well, by devoting a few hours at night to trading. One of the things that makes Forex more attractive than the stock market is the ability to trade 24 hours a day, so you can trade when you are able and want to trade, rather than being constrained by business hours. That said, scalping on a limited time frame might limit your profits, too.

Chapter 7: Technical vs. Fundamental Analysis

After reviewing the strategies that are used in Forex trading, we will discuss the tools that are used in Forex trading. We are going to keep it relatively simple because frankly, it's not necessary to overcomplicate things. The main tools that we are going to focus on are tools that will help you keep track of pricing trends and help you find signals of trend reversals.

The first thing to consider is technical vs. fundamental analysis. If you are someone who has done trading on the stock market, you will have some idea of what these two concepts are about. In the Forex markets, there are some general similarities and some differences. When it comes to technical analysis, there are more similarities to be found than differences, however.

Technical analysis involves the use of tools that can be applied to any financial instrument that is traded on a marketplace. The tools of technical analysis can be used to get information about trading volume, pricing trends, and pricing trend reversals. There are three main tools that are used by most traders. The first tool that is used is the candlestick charts. Candlestick charts divide up a graph of pricing of a financial asset into short time intervals, using a graphical representation (in the form of a "candlestick") that gives you pricing information for each time interval. The candlestick will let you know what the high and low prices were for the time interval, what the open and closing prices were for the time interval, and whether the closing price finished above or below the opening price, indicating whether traders were "bullish" or "bearish" on the financial asset for the given time period. Moreover, candlesticks help you see how trends are developing and possibly reversing. We are going to talk about candlesticks more in a bit.

The other tools that are frequently used include moving averages, which smooth out pricing data by averaging them, Bollinger bands, which help you see the one standard deviation pricing rage for a financial asset, and the relative strength indicator which helps you determine whether an asset is "overbought" or "oversold." You can also look at the average pip movement.

What technical analysis comes down to, is it's a set of tools that helps you determine the buildup of trends and pricing shifts as supply and demand for a given financial asset changes in the marketplace. Technical analysis is not concerned with what is causing those price movements, or even what the underlying financial security is.

Fundamental analysis is an entirely different ballgame. As we discussed in the introductory chapter of the book, fundamental analysis in the stock market looks at the financial health of the company, its management team, and studies the market the company is in.

Fundamental analysis for Forex markets is far broader, and actually quite a bit simpler. The main components of fundamental analysis when currencies are the subject of interest are the interest rate of the central bank, the interest rate of the central bank for the country that is the other party to a given currency pair (and so we are really considering the interest rate differential between the two countries), and the overall economic health of each country.

Other things play an important role in fundamental analysis, and we've mentioned some of them in the previous chapters. For example, the exports that a country relies on are important, and therefore changes in commodity prices are something that needs to be considered. GDP growth rates, unemployment, and other factors are things to look at where fundamental analysis is concerned. If one member of a currency pair is performing in a much better way in comparison to the other when it comes to these metrics, that can mean that it is the better choice for the currency pair.

As we have also alluded to earlier in the book, news events are important to pay attention to. You want to look for both positive and negative news events, but a bad event can drive investors out of a country, such as a terrorist attack, or a political upheaval. It's important to keep up with the news even if such events seem unlikely in current circumstances; many quiet years can go by before the international situation deteriorates or becomes chaotic. A large-scale terrorist attack could hurt an economy or drive tourism away, at least temporarily. An economic recession can also cause problems if it is localized to one country. As we mentioned earlier, in many cases, if these kinds of problems are widespread, many people move to the perceived safety of the Swiss Franc, which has proven immune to such upheavals.

Factors to Consider in Technical Analysis

Candlestick Charts

Now, let's turn our attention to the specifics of technical analysis. The first tool of technical analysis that a new trader needs to learn is candlestick charts. A candlestick is a representation of price movement over a specific time period that you set for your chart. For example, you can set the time period to a minute, 5 minutes, or even one day. This is the trading session. The candlestick will have a body, and two upper and lower shadows or wicks.

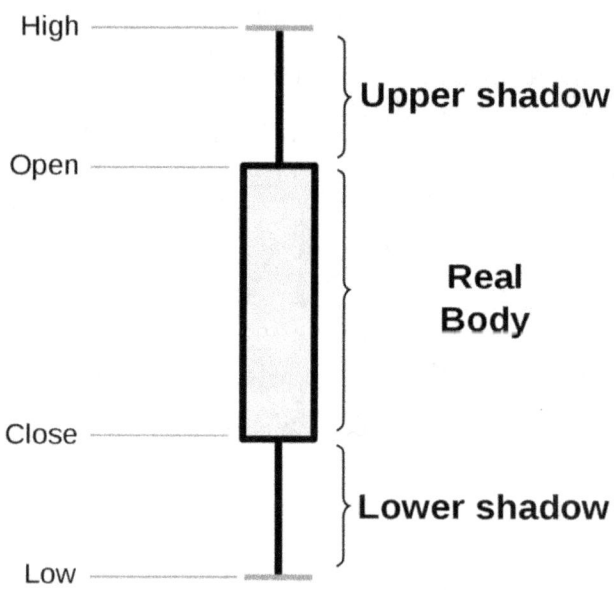

The upper wick represents the high price for the trading session. The lower wick represents the low price for the candlestick. The body of the candlestick represents the opening and closing prices for the trading session. There are two general types of candlesticks. They can be bullish, in which case they represent a trading session where prices were pushed upward. In that case, the top of the candlestick body is the closing price for the trading session, while the bottom of the candlestick would be the opening price for the trading session. Bullish candlesticks are either solid green in color or outlined green on trading charts. If the chart is black and white, the candlestick will be an outline for the bullish trading session.

If the asset price dropped during the trading session, then you have a bearish candlestick. On charts with white backgrounds, they are colored red—and in most cases with charts, with black backgrounds. Bearish candlesticks are colored white—on a black-and-white chart. A bearish candlestick will have a solid black body. For a bearish candlestick, the top of the candlestick body represents the opening price for the trading session, while the bottom of the candlestick body is the closing price – so this represents a case where the price dropped. In both cases (bearish and bullish), the meaning of the wicks or shadows extended out from the candlesticks is the same.

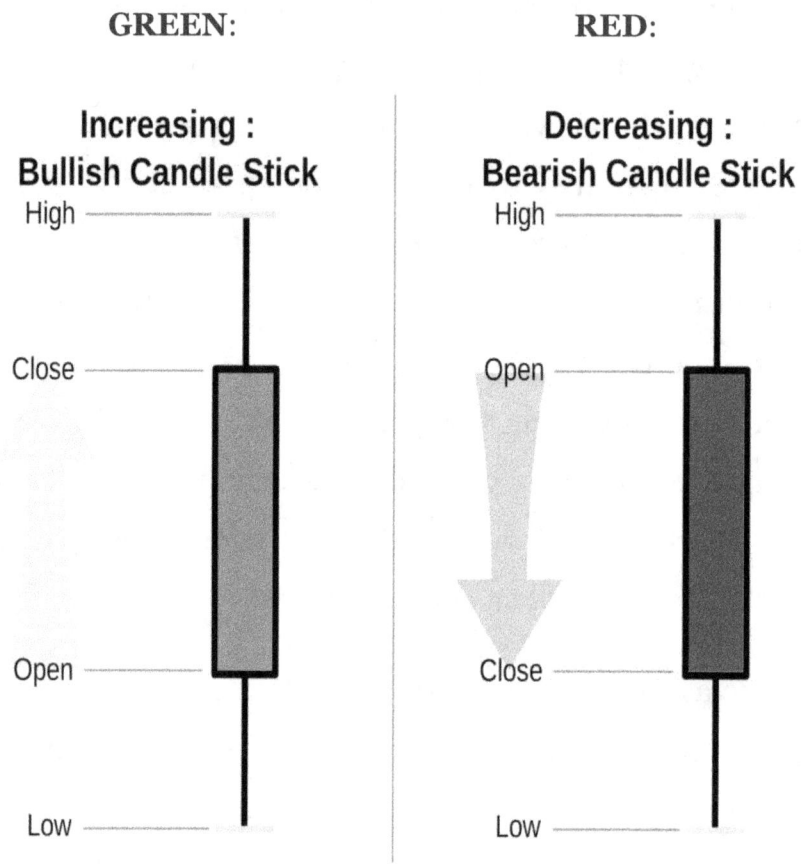

The trader studies candlestick patterns in order to look for signals that trends are going to reverse. A candlestick pattern, by itself, is not a reason to enter or exit a trade.

The trader will "confirm" the signal seen in the candlesticks with at least two other methods that we will discuss below.

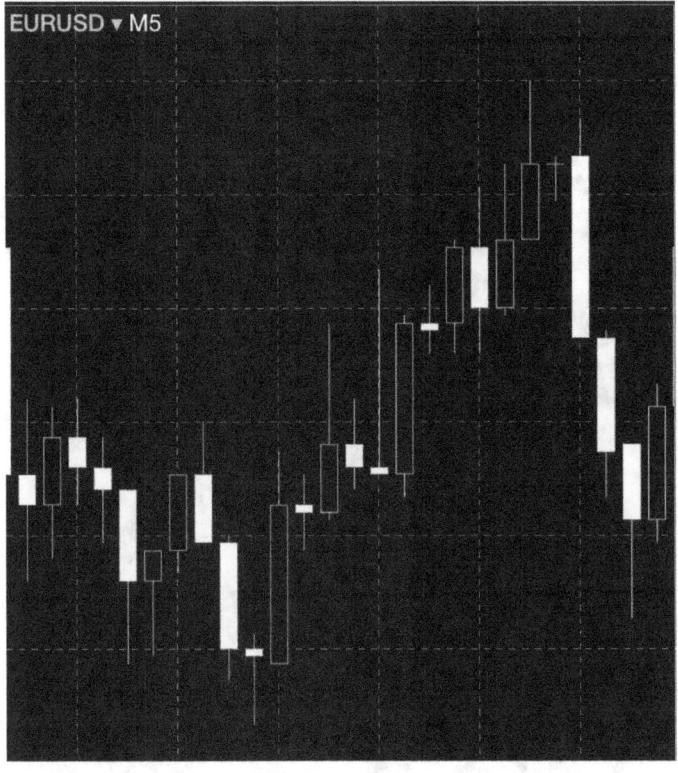

Many trading platforms use black backgrounds for Forex charts. In this case, the white candlesticks are bearish, and the green outlined candlesticks are bullish.

There are many patterns that you need to become familiar with in order to be successful using candlestick charts to help you make the right trades. The first thing to look for is called an engulfing pattern. This happens when the candlestick of one type (bearish or bullish) is followed by a candlestick of the opposite type. The second candlestick will have a much larger body, indicating that the price was driven upwards by a large amount during the trading session. The candlestick would "engulf" or completely cover the previous candlestick. This type of pattern is shown below. It indicates a coming upward trend in price.

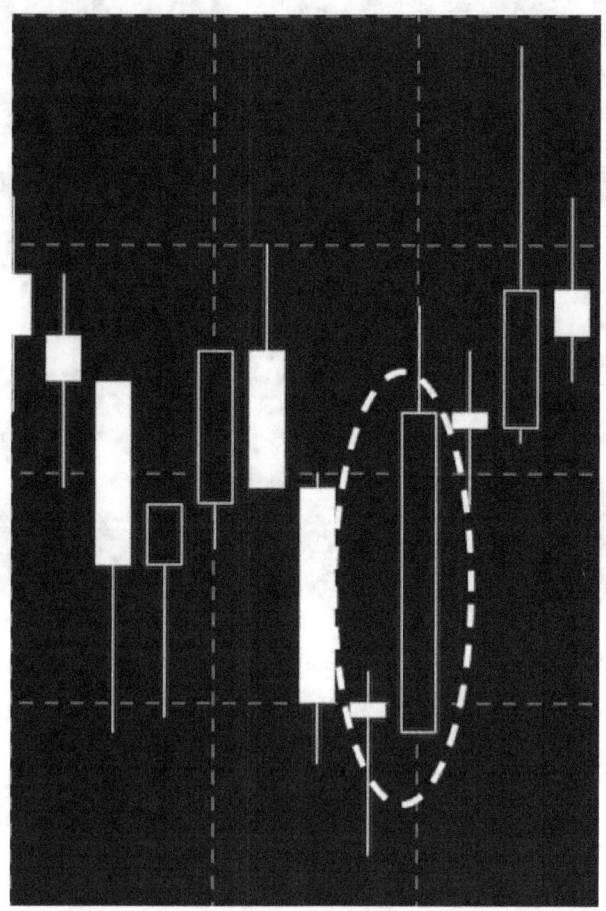

The next pattern that we are going to look at is called "three white soldiers." The name is historical and comes from the old black-and-white charts where the bullish candlesticks would be white with black outlines. Today we might call it "three green soldiers." This is three bullish candlesticks in a row, with higher highs in succession. This indicates a coming upward trend. This is shown below.

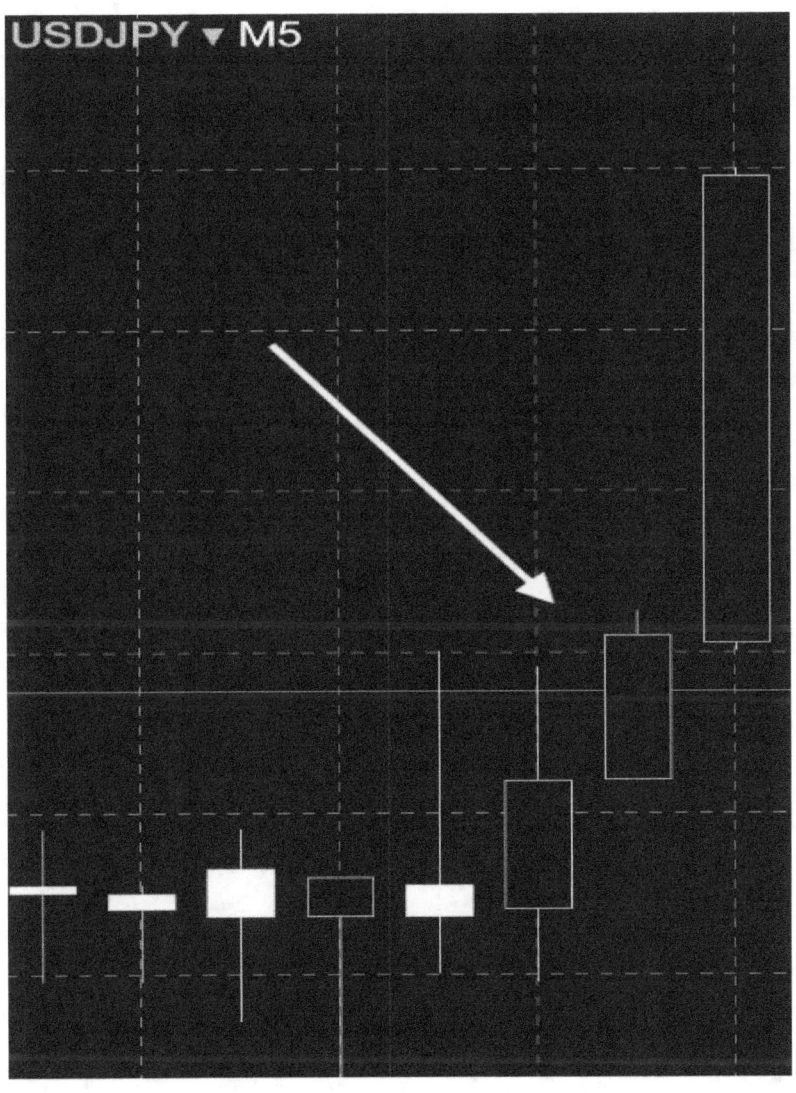

Next, we come to a "doji" indecision candle. This candle has a thin line for a body, indicating that the opening and closing prices for the trading session were the same.

The candle will also have long wicks, indicating that the prices were pushed up high and down low during the trading session, but they ended up back at the opening price. This is the "indecision," traders were neither bullish or bearish during the trading session.

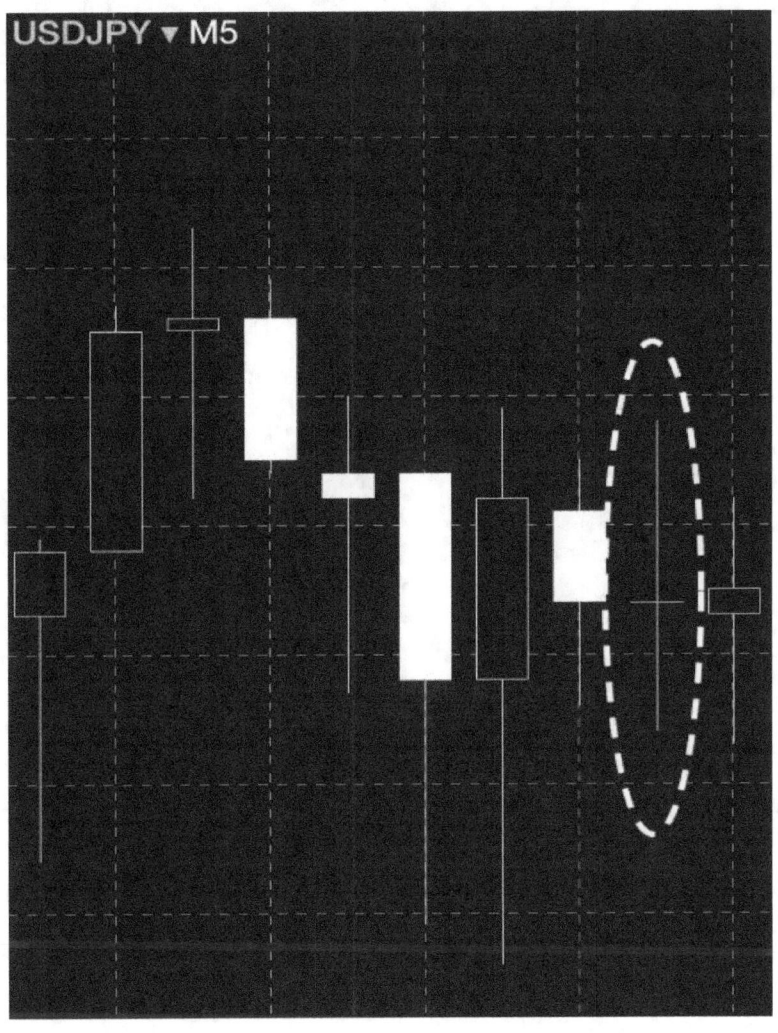

Another signal that an upward trend in price is coming is called an inverted hammer. In this case, you will see a bullish candlestick with a relatively narrow body, but with a long upward wick, indicating the prices were pushed up high during the trading session. Even though the high was not maintained, the price closed higher than the open, and the opening price is the low price for the trading session. It should be confirmed using technical indicators like a moving average crossover (see below).

R = RED   G = GREEN

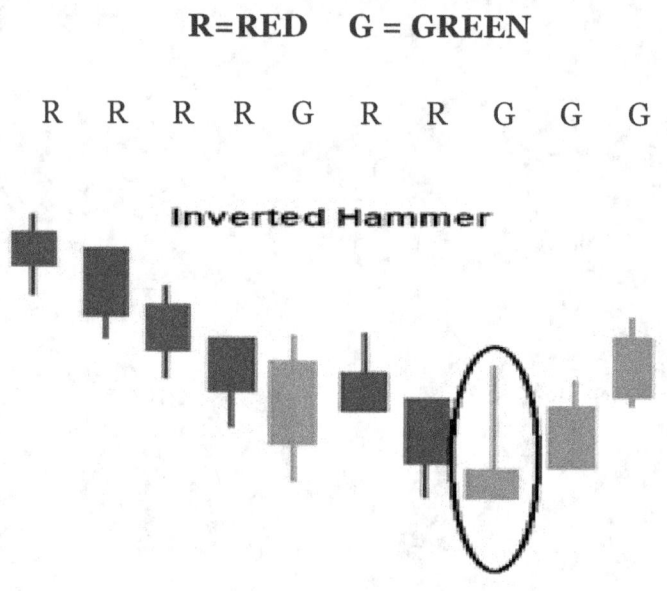

A hammer is this pattern in reverse, and if a hammer occurs at the top of an uptrend, this may indicate a coming downward trend in price.

There is also a pattern known as a shooting star. In this case, there is a bearish candle in the form of an inverted hammer, appearing at the top of an uptrend. So it will have a long wick shooting upward, the "shooting" part of the star, but it will close at a lower price than the open.

Shooting Star

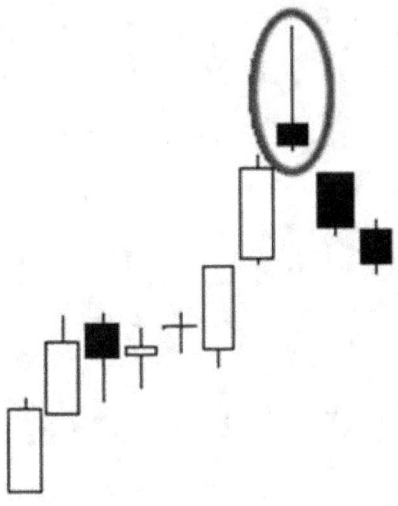

The same types of patterns that form with bullish candlesticks can form with bearish candlesticks as well. In these cases, they indicate a coming downward trend in prices. For example, we can have three bearish candlesticks in a row, indicating declining prices, with lower lows for each closing price. This is called three black crows, a historical reference to the time when the charts were black and white, and the bearish candlesticks were solid black in color.

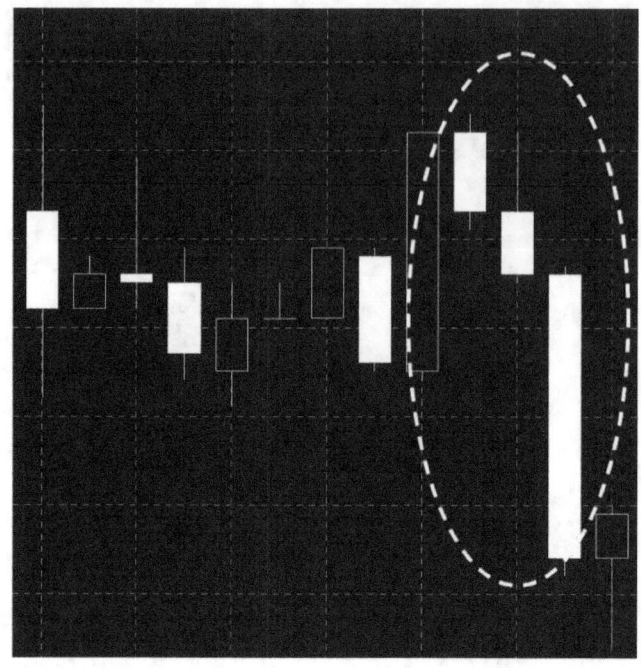

Next, we consider an evening star. This is a pattern that can indicate a coming downtrend. When there is an evening star, you first see a large upward push in prices with a large bullish candlestick. This is followed by a hammer that is a bearish hammer, so the price closed below the open. That indicates that although the price had been pushed up, it wasn't possible to keep finding buyers.

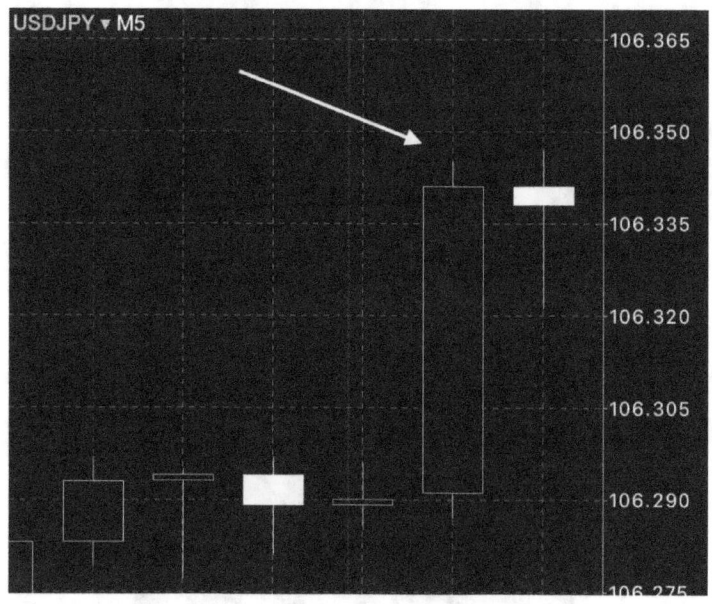

The abandoned baby pattern appears at the end of a downtrend. In this case, there is a large bearish candle that ends a streak of bearish candles. Then, there is a doji indecision candle, indicating that sellers are not coming to the table anymore. This is followed by a bullish candle indicating a buying spree is coming up:

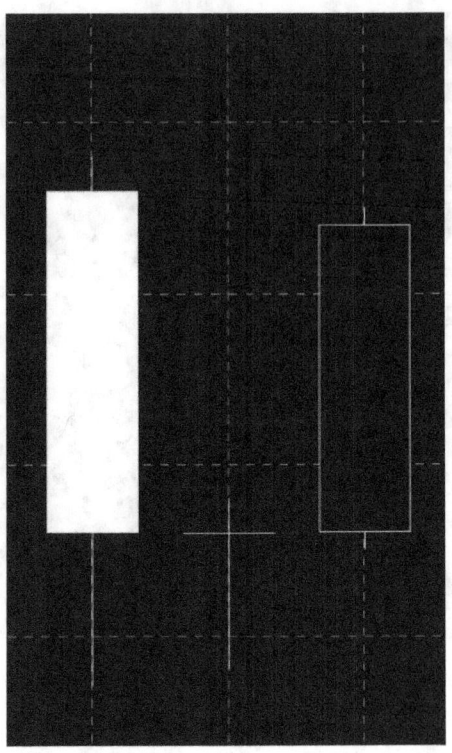

The terms bullish and bearish used with candlesticks come from the stock market, where rising prices are desirable. Keep in mind that on the Forex markets, rising or falling prices are not framed in the same way, because you might be betting on the secondary currency and so you are hoping for falling prices.

So for the Forex markets, bullish means that the primary currency is rising against the secondary currency, while bearish means the secondary currency is rising against the primary currency. So whether something is really "bullish" or not depends on what side of the trade you are on.

There are many other candlestick patterns that you can use. An entire book could be written on this topic, and we don't have space to cover them all. But you should be educated on them all before you start trading, so you should look for videos, articles, and even Udemy courses about candlesticks online.

Moving Averages

Moving averages simply compute the average of a recent set of prices at each point, and generate a curve from it. Data from financial markets is often quite noisy, with many ups and downs that are essentially meaningless when you are looking for longer-term trends. A moving average gives you a smooth curve for the prices.

However, the real way that moving averages are used is to look for trend reversals. In order to do this, you will need to have two moving averages together on the same chart. This will include moving averages that track different numbers of time periods. A common choice is to use a 9-period moving average and a 20-period moving average.

Once you have your moving averages selected, you will look for the curves to cross. When the short period moving average crosses above the long period moving average, this is called a *golden cross*. That means that the price is going to be increasing, that is it's the start of an upward trend. In the example below, the short-term moving average (the green curve) crosses above the long-term moving average (the red line), giving a golden cross pattern.

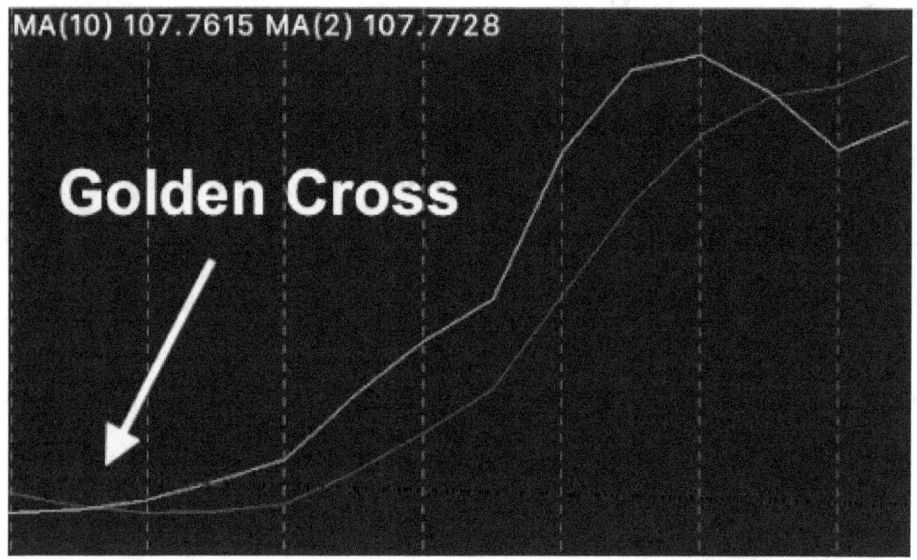

In the example below, the green line is a short-term moving average. The red line is the long-term moving average. The green line has crossed below the long-term moving average, indicating that there is a coming downtrend in price. This is known as a death cross.

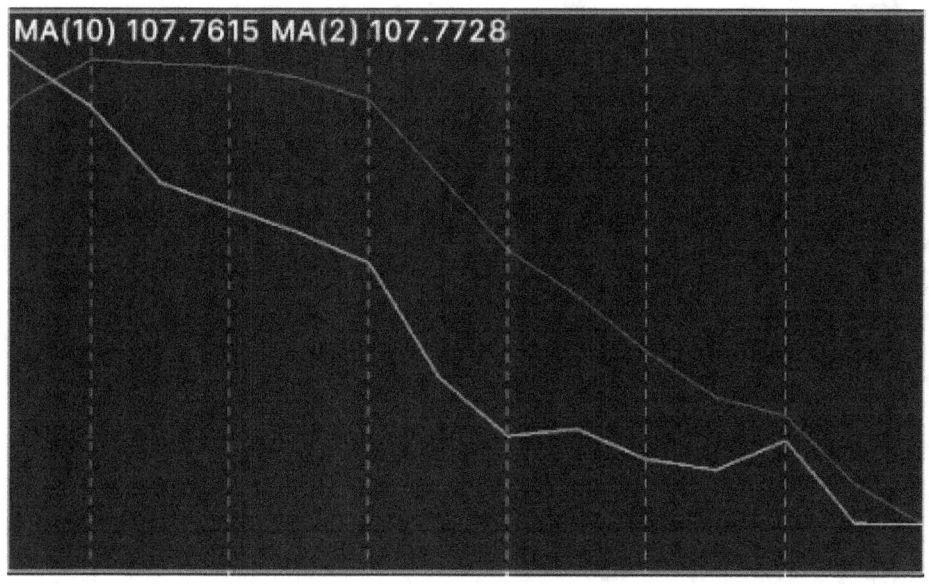

MA(10) 107.7615 MA(2) 107.7728

There are many different types of moving averages that you can use. A simple moving average simply averages the values, using the number of periods given. The problem with this type of moving average, especially for long-term moving averages, is that this will give the same weight to all prices. For example, suppose that you were tracking a daily chart, and you had a 20 period moving average. If it is a simple moving average, the price 20 days ago would have the same weight in the calculation as the price yesterday. Obviously, this would not be an accurate way to look at the data. Over a 20-day period, fundamentals may have changed, for example. And just looking at speculating and trends, the speculating that occurred 20 days ago isn't as relevant.

For this reason, most Forex traders use exponential moving averages. The details don't concern us here, but exponential moving averages weight the data. So yesterday's price has more weight than the price 5 days ago, which in turn has more weight than the price 20 days ago. There are other weighted moving averages, such as the Hull moving average, but the exponential moving average is probably the most popular.

Strength Indicators

Another technical indicator you may want to use is the relative strength indicator. This indicator helps you get an idea if a financial asset is overbought or oversold. This helps you determine the momentum in a trend. When we say an asset is overbought, this means that the price has been pushed too high with respect to the actual value of the asset. In other words, the price is pushed higher than the fundamentals would indicate is valid. When this happens, the price can continue increasing, but the momentum of the price increase is probably going to peter out, and the price trend will peak out and eventually reverse. At this point, in short order, people holding the asset are going to recognize that it's overpriced, and they will start dumping it on the market so they can exit their positions at a relative high pricing point.

This can happen on the downside as well. In this case, we are talking about an oversold asset. This means the price that is driven down lower than the fundamentals would indicate a valid price. At this point, momentum to push the price down is going to be decreasing, even if, for a while, prices continue to drop. This probably indicates that a trend reversal is coming, and prices will start rising again. It's just a matter of time before buyers recognize that the asset has now become available at a bargain price, and so they will start moving in to buy the asset and push prices back up.

The RSI runs over 0-100. There are different conventions used with the relative strength indicator, but the standard is using 70-80 as the cutoff point for overbought. That is, if the RSI is above 70 or 80 (70 is probably too conservative), you should consider a rising price trend as overbought, and it will probably reverse soon. For oversold conditions, and RSI less than 20 is typically used.

Bollinger Bands

The next technical indicator that you should at least be aware of is called Bollinger bands. This is a more complicated indicator that brings three pieces of information together. It consists of three curves. In the center, there is a moving average curve. You can set the type of moving average that you want to use, but by default, it will be a simple moving average. There are curves above and below the moving average that show the one standard deviations above and below the moving average. This helps you to determine levels of support and resistance as well as signs that a breakout may occur.

During a timeframe that the financial asset is ranging, it will have price fluctuations that are contained within the Bollinger bands. Therefore, if you are buying a currency pair, you can wait for the price to drop to the lower Bollinger (or alternatively, you can buy when the price touches the moving average if there are other signs it will begin rising in price). Then, you sell when the price moves to the upper Bollinger band.

When the candlesticks move outside one of the outer Bollinger bands, this can be a sign of a coming breakout. If the wicks, or especially the body, go above the upper-level Bollinger band, this can be taken as an indicator that the price is going to start moving upward, until it establishes a new higher level of pricing support.

Alternatively, you can look for instances of the candlesticks going below the lower Bollinger band, which can indicate the possibility of a break to the downside in prices, which can be a start of a new downward trend.

The Depth Line

You may also take a look at the market in-depth in order to determine the supply and demand for a given currency pair. This tells you the number of open buy-and-sell orders for the currency pair. The larger the number of buying and selling orders, the more the depth of the market. The importance of this value is the higher the depth line, the more liquidity there is in the market for the given currency pair. It will also give you an idea of how likely it is that your order will be filled in a timely fashion at a given price. Of course, for major currency pairs such as the EUR/USD, liquidity is never going to be an issue. However, even in that case, you can use market depth so that you can see how many open orders there are at different price points. There will be an ask volume and a bid volume. The ask is the asking price from sellers, and the bid is the price that buyers are bidding and willing to pay. You can also see the total ask less total bid on your charts so that you can get an estimate of how different these values are – giving an indication of how quickly orders are going to be filled. If there is a large difference in value between the bid and ask prices, then that can indicate that there is going to be some difficulty in filling orders. On the other hand, if the difference is small, orders will be filled quickly.

Factors to Consider in Fundamental Analysis

In this section, we are going to briefly examine the main factors you should consider when using fundamental analysis as a part of your toolkit to determine which currencies you want to invest in.

Interest Rates

Interest rates are an important metric to consider. There are many factors that will determine the strength of a currency, but all things considered equal, higher interest rates mean the currency is going to be more in demand, and therefore it will rise against other currencies. If the interest rate in the United States rises, outside investors will be more interested in buying bonds and other interest producing assets inside the United States, and they are going to need dollars to do it. Therefore, this means that the demand for dollars will rise, and prices will be pushed up. But the key thing for Forex is the fact that currencies are traded in pairs, and so you also have to consider one interest rate against the other. So fundamental analysis will, in part, involve knowing global interest rates, or at least the interest rates of the majors.

Inflation

Inflation is another key factor. A high inflation rate means that inside the country, the currency is losing value. High inflation rates may make investing in the currency of a given country a bad proposition. Once again, when looking at a given currency pair, you are going to want to make relative comparisons for the inflation rates in the two countries.

GDP Growth Rates

When the GDP growth rate for a company is strong, this is going to attract more investment, generally speaking. Of course, there are many factors involved. If inflation is out of control, then high GDP growth rates may not be that attractive. But if all other indicators are good, a solid GDP growth rate is going to bring people to the table, which means that demand for the currency will be high.

Unemployment

The unemployment rate is another indicator of the health of the economy. High unemployment rates will make the currency unattractive, while lower unemployment rates are going to make the currency more attractive. Again, this is something that has to be seen in a relative context; you are going to compare the unemployment rate to the other partner in the currency pair. You will also want to look at the labor force participation rate if this data is available, as well as the number of people working full-time or part-time.

Trade

Trade issues can be important, too. When there is a lot of trade, there is also a lot of exchange of currency. For example, consider Japan, dollars flowing into the country need to be exchanged for Japanese Yen so that Japanese companies can use their profits at home. Besides trade, you will also want to look at any monetary flows between countries by large corporations, which eventually can mean having to exchange the currency into the local variety.

Chapter 8: Your Trading Plan

While it's possible just to start trading and have some success, most people are going to need to have a plan in order to be successful. In order to increase the probability that you profit from your trading, having a plan is strongly recommended. Having a plan means setting goals and knowing where you are going, as well as knowing how much risk you can tolerate. We will address these issues in this chapter.

Structuring a Trading Plan

The first thing to include in your trading plan is your overall goal. Are you planning to get to a point where you can trade Forex full-time? If so, you need to be specific about how much money you need to earn in order to accomplish this. From here, you need to determine what lot sizes to trade, as well as how many trades you are going to need to do on average in order to reach your goals.

Part of this is going to be knowing the average pip movement for the currency pairs you want to trade. Of course, that value might change over time, and in any given trade, it's seldom going to be on the average. But it will give you an idea of how many trades and how large an investment you need to make in order to meet the income needs you are aiming for.

You also need to figure out how long you are going to give yourself in order to reach your goals. You should set sub-goals along the way so that you are making progress in small steps. It's not going to be possible for most people to go from starting out as a beginner to making $60k a year in the first month of trading. It will take time to build up to it, and mistakes are going to be made along the way that will inevitably lead to losses. When starting out, you are going to have to chalk those up to learning experiences, and also acknowledge the fact that losses are part of the business, and even the best traders are going to have losses on some trades.

Set specific dates to reach specific income targets. These don't have to be rules written in stone. If you fail to meet them, regroup and adjust with new dates. The point is to hold yourself accountable for meeting specific goals and trying to reach them.

You should also determine the strategy you want to follow and how many hours a day you will devote to trading. Also, log a trading schedule, even if you are doing part-time swing trading and only working an hour a night on it. The more you stick to a schedule, the more likely you are going to find success.

Keep a Trading Journal

You should also keep a trading journal so that you know just what you are doing. The human mind has a capacity for self-deception, and people will have a habit of remembering their wins while ignoring trading losses. Record each trade along with how much you earned or lost on the trade, and keep a running balance for each month. That way, you will know exactly where you stand, and you will have a record that you can use to go over your mistakes and make adjustments.

Goals and Budgets

You should not trade if you are getting yourself in a situation where a loss would wipe you out financially, and put you in a position where you have to scramble to find a job or hustle to borrow money in order to eat or pay the bills. Determine how much money you can afford to lose – and limit your Forex trading to that by setting that as your budget. Also, keep track of your goals and set realistic goals. Think in terms of baby steps that add up over time. You should not think of trying to hit a big win right away.

Stop-Loss and Take Profit Orders

One of the most important principles of disciplined trading is having stop-loss and take profit orders. Most brokers allow you to place these automatically so that you are not getting too involved in your trades emotionally and making stupid decisions. Stop-loss orders will automatically exit the position for you if you lose a given amount on a trade. These are a must to have so that you can protect yourself against a margin call. Without a stop-loss order, you might find yourself in a position of having your entire account wiped out in a matter of minutes or even seconds.

A take profit order allows you to take profits at a reasonable level for a given trade. You need to set things up so that you know how much you want to earn for each trade that you enter. Then, set up a take profit order to automatically exit the trade if your profit level is reached. Don't sit there hoping that things will move in your favor so that you make even more money. Many times, if you do this, you will find yourself holding on too long, and you will end up losing on trades that you should have walked away from with profits.

Chapter 9: Forex Trading Secrets

In this chapter, we will cover some tips for success for Forex traders. You can also look at this as mistakes you need to avoid.

Stick to One Trading Style

As we said earlier, it's possible to use swing trading as a training ground so that you can become a day trader later—but generally speaking, people who are all over the map doing different methods are not going to end up being successful. If you want to become a scalper, as an example, you should devote sufficient time and energy to it and study it thoroughly so that you can become an expert. If you are interested in doing trend trading, then stick with that.

Start with a Demo Account

Spend some time trading using a demo account. That doesn't excite people, especially if they are anxious. But it's a good idea to do it, so you can see in real-time how trades you would have placed would work out. You can also get some practical experience doing trading – and hopefully backing up your trades with some technical analysis – without risking money.

Stick to a Limited Number of Currency Pairs

A focused trader is going to have more success than someone who is all over the map. No matter what currency pairs you find you prefer, you should stick to a small number of them in your trading. I'd recommend using 2-3 currency pairs in your trades. This gives you space to learn the currencies in-depth so that you can increase your odds of trading success. When you spread yourself thin, your knowledge and experience with different currencies are going to be thin as well, and this will limit your abilities to make consistent profits.

Always Use Stop-Loss Orders and Limit Risk

Don't be tempted to manage your trades on the loss side manually. Use a stop-loss order so that you automatically get out of your trades. Things can move very fast on the Forex markets, and if you don't have a stop-loss order, then you are going to put yourself in danger of wiping out your account and possibly facing a margin call. For a total amount to risk, you should risk no more than 3% of the total cash in your account on a single trade. That doesn't mean you only put 3% in total to the trade; what this means is that you set your stop-loss order so that the amount you would lose would be 3% of your total account.

Don't Trade Based on Emotion

Trading based on emotion is a major mistake. Panic can set in when it appears you might face losses, and greed can set in if you see an opportunity for large gains. It's very easy to let emotion get the best of you, and unfortunately, many beginners fall into this trap. The way to avoid it is to stick to using stop-loss and take profit orders.

Don't Neglect Fundamental Analysis

While many traders get deep into technical analysis, you should keep your eye on the fundamentals, too. Do this even if you are a short-term trader. After all, when you are day trading, announcements about various economic factors can lead to large price movements. So don't be blind to it. Keep up with fundamental analysis for the currencies that you trade. This is another reason to avoid trading a large number of currencies.

Be Informed and Educated

The fact that you are reading this book is a good sign. You have taken the time out in order to actually learn something about Forex trading. You should not stop here. The more informed and educated you are about trading, the more likely you are to be successful. Keep educating yourself by reading books, articles, and watching as many educational videos as you can.

Stick to Your Plan

Don't go through the trouble of developing a trading plan and then ignore it! Develop your trading plan and stick to it. Follow it for at least three months. If it is not working out, but you are still determined to become a successful Forex trader, then redo the plan at that time and make adjustments—but whatever you do, actually follow the plan in your trading.

Conclusion

Thank you for making it through to the end of *Forex Trading Strategy: How to Invest with the Simplest and Most Profitable Strategy to Make Money in Trading Stocks, Options, Forex, and ETFs in 2019/2020 in Just 30 Minutes Per Day*! Let's hope it was informative and able to provide you with all of the tools you need to achieve your goals—whatever they may be.

The next step is to open a Forex trading account and spend a couple of weeks trading with a demo account while you continue educating yourself about Forex. Then, once you are comfortable, start executing some real trades!

Forex trading is not for everyone, but if it interests you, I hope that this book will help guide you to success.

Finally, if you found this book useful in any way, a review on Amazon is always appreciatcd!

Also**, MY FREE GIFT TO YOU**: If you buy the OPTION TRADING BOOK that I wrote, I will give you 2 swing trading audiobooks completely for free!

Disclaimer

Please note that *Forex Trading Strategy*, Jim Livermore, and anyone related to creating this book are not to be held liable for any results that the reader may gain from trading using these strategies. This book is designed for educational purposes only and should be viewed as such by the reader. Any action the reader takes on the information in this book is solely the responsibility and liability of the reader themselves, no one else.

My FREE Gift for You

If you buy my other title, *"Options Trading"* I will give you the 2 *"Forex Trading Strategy + Options Trading"* Audiobooks 100% FREE! Options trading allows you to leverage the power of controlling hundreds of shares of stock, but without actually having to buy the stock. Options trading is exciting, and when you read this book you're going to find out why. It's one of the easiest and most fun and yet challenging ways to make profits on the stock market. If you want to get started earning an independent income from trading, don't hesitate to download this book *today.*

What Should I Read Next?

Swing Trading for Beginners: The 2019/20 Valuable Swing Trading Guide for Learning How to Improve Your Trading Results and Your Finances with the Best Low-Risk Approaches

Swing Trading Option: The Ultimate Trading Guide to Discover Safe and Profitable Trading Strategies for Generating Fast and Secure Profits and Rapid Growth for Your Finances

Stocks Option Trading: Learn and Understand How Everything Works and What Pitfalls you MUST Avoid as a Beginner. Learn How Top Investors Lower Their Cost Basis Using Stock Options

Stock Options Trading Strategies: The Best Step-by-Step Guide to Learn How to Trade Stocks and Discover How TOP Traders Invest. The Best Strategies to Help You Create Your Financial Freedom

Options Trading: The Best Beginner's Guide with All the Essential Information an Investor Needs on How the Options Market Works and How to Start Trading Options in 2019/2020.

www.ingramcontent.com/pod-product-compliance
Lightning Source LLC
Chambersburg PA
CBHW070338220526
45467CB00001B/160